MARY PAUSE

Marypause

Copyright © Mary Coustas 2025

Mary Coustas asserts the moral right to be identified as the author of *Marypause* and all associated products.

First published in Australia in 2025 by
ITHACA HOUSE PUBLISHING
PO Box 404, Coogee, NSW 2034, Australia

ISBN 978-1-7643213-2-7 (Paperback)
ISBN 978-1-7643213-3-4 (Hardcover)
ISBN 978-1-7643213-1-0 (Epub)

All rights reserved. No part of this publication may be reproduced or transmitted, copied, stored in a retrieval system, distributed or otherwise made available by any person or entity (including Google, Amazon or similar organisations), in any form (electronic, digital, optical, mechanical or otherwise), or by any means (photocopying, recording, scanning or otherwise) without prior written permission from the publisher, except in the case of brief quotations embodied in critical reviews and certain other non-commercial uses permitted by copyright law.

For permissions, contact: hello@marypause.com.au

 A catalogue record for this book is available from the National Library of Australia

Editor: Chris Anastassiades
Book cover design: Jenny Liu
Author front cover photograph: Cybele Malinowski
Author back cover photograph: Nicholas Samartis
Produced for the author by: exlibris.com.au
Published for global distribution by: Julie Postance, iinspire media

Printed by IngramSpark

DISCLAIMER
The characters, incidents, and dialogue in this memoir are drawn from the author's own experience. Names and identifying details may have been changed to protect privacy.

MARY PAUSE

MARY COUSTAS

ITHACA HOUSE PUBLISHING
Sydney | Melbourne | Athens

DEDICATION

For Jamie and Nathalie

May the magnificence of your miraculous female bodies amuse you more than bamboozle you.

I couldn't love you both more.

My heart has stretch marks.

*

To Chris — my creative soul mate

Everything is possible and funnier with you there.
You champion my ambition, mission and gender — always.
Thank you for being born with so much heart and talent.

And no doubt, some ovaries too.

*

To George — my husband, playmate and dairy-loving punching bag.

I want to thank you for… ah… can I get back to you on that?

Actually, everything!! Your passion to make things better is equal parts exhausting and inspiring.
Thank you for insisting that you're always right.

I LOVE you, Georgie.

"In a game of
rock, paper, scissors.
The body always wins."

MC

INTRODUCTION

I SEE FUNNY EVERYWHERE

There isn't a moment in my life — and I've had some pretty dark ones — where I have failed to unearth the funny.

Laughter is my oxygen; I can't live without it. None of us can. It brings us relief, unites us, and provides much-needed perspective. Throughout my losses, disappointments, heartbreaks and humiliations, there has always been something comical; a moment, a feeling, a joke that comes to the surface and helps soothe the pain.

It isn't always obvious. There have been times and incidents where I've really had to dig deep and get forensic about finding something to even smile about, but somehow, I always manage.

Then along came menopause.

That unexpected retirement party for my ovaries was no party. It crept up on me like a sinister physiological swat team. Each member, one by one, manifested themselves in various parts of my body: robbing, fogging and dehydrating me physically and at the same time psychologically kidnapping my optimism, my personality and my patience.

So many of the symptoms stayed hidden, lurking camouflaged

among the other painful experiences of my past, the other times when my body was under hormonal siege. And because of that, it was completely invisible to me.

My body felt like it was under new management, and I didn't have the email login.

How can you find the funny when you can't even identify what exactly you're supposed to be laughing at?

For whatever reason I didn't see menopause coming. Even though I was aware it was one of those inevitable events in every woman's life, it still completely caught me off-guard.

Like many of us, I bought into the dangerous narrative that it was a "fuss about nothing." Just a bit of dryness and maybe some night-sweats as the hormonal train leaves the station.

Little did I know that I was tied to the tracks and that hormonal crash was going to run me over, disrupt my whole life and leave me physically and psychologically devastated.

Even scarier, I was clueless that what I was experiencing was due to menopause. I assumed it was just ageing or some 'other thing' that happens to women. Because a lot seems to happen — and keep happening — to women's bodies. It wasn't denial. It was absence.

Menopause had been almost completely erased from the conversation. And I, like millions of women, inherited that silence.

Our bodies are like one continuous episode of *The White Lotus*. Just when you check in at a nice resort, looking forward to a relaxing time away from the pressures of the real world with the people you love, someone finds a body at the beach, you discover your husband is having an affair and the sex-worker paid by the guy in the next room is singing in the lounge and somehow blackmailing you.

And you just deal with it. Like you dealt with unwanted hair sprouting in odd places, period pain, the pungent aroma of adolescence, pregnancy, childbirth, etc. You learn to manage the symptoms and just keep going.

But for me, menopause was completely unmanageable.

The physical price of diminishing hormones had definitely taken its ugly toll on how my body functioned, more to the point — didn't function.

But even more challenging for me was the psychological overwhelm. The combination of both of those things impacted every aspect of my life: my marriage, my friendships, my work, my body, my sleep — or lack thereof.

Everyday ordinary things became unbearable; the traffic, inane conversations at the school gate, bad takeaway coffee, back pain, listening to the symptoms of man flu related in painstaking detail, navigating online payments — did I mention traffic?

My response to all that was to retreat. It was the complete opposite to how I had functioned for a lifetime.

Menopause alienated me from my body and separated me from my people.

That only made it harder, because if I have an addiction, it's to one thing, human beings, especially the ones I love.

Long story long… everything felt impossibly, confusingly hard and acutely painful.

Menopause overwhelmed me and froze me into inaction. It was like I'd been the victim of a hormonal hit-job that put me right in the centre of a mid-life demolition.

It filled me with anxiety, uncertainty, and fear and I couldn't move myself to do anything about it. I became unrecognisable; paralysed, brain-fogged Mary, riddled with ignorance and devoid of hormones.

Then one morning, when I could barely lift myself out of bed, when the heaviness of my chest could no longer be ignored, and when my tears seemed to be auditioning — yet again — for *Niagara Falls: The Non-Musical*, it struck me! I finally knew what was happening.

How could I have missed the myriad clues?

I slid sideways out of bed, somehow got to my feet, shuffled into the kitchen and blurted out to my confused husband, "It's menopause! It must be menopause!"

Finally, I'd cracked it.

Well, I'd been cracking it a lot at every small thing, but this was the good kind of "cracking it" like when they solve a cold case on TV. The culprit had been found. And the culprit was… me.

Well, what was happening to me.

In an instant, the world opened up and relief was in sight. I inhaled books, articles and websites. I discovered Instagram accounts by a plethora of informed, inspiring women stepping to the fore to help — a number that's growing every day.

It was there I found answers and people that I didn't know existed. Expert doctors that diagnosed menopausal women every day and yet for some reason, had difficulty when it came to diagnosing themselves. Further proof that this blind-spot exists in so many women, just like it did in me.

I read about the vast litany of symptoms, some known and many that were not. I discovered treatments and people that were on a mission to change things for the better. Thanks to them, and the resources they provide, menopause is moving from something we have had to suffer through quietly in the shadows, to something we no longer need to face alone.

Suddenly, I went from tired to inspired. Inspired to shed light on an issue that plunged me into isolation and darkness. To detoxify an archaic taboo with laughter. To, along with so many others, help open the menopause closet door once and for all.

To do my bit. Just as others were compelled to.

And this book, *Marypause*, is the first part of my contribution.

My physical story, anti-climaxing with menopause.

Part reflection, part memoir, it has allowed me to explore my experience of menopause — and why it hit me so hard — by looking at it in the context of my whole physical life. The complicated, painful, embarrassing and perplexing parts of being a woman. And the funny and fantastic parts too.

Its aim is to explore how powerful and powerless we can all be and to act as a reminder that far too often, we're not the ones running the show but that we're at the mercy of a bunch of mysterious, elusive and sometimes unreliable things called hormones.

This book became a place where I could talk about those things. To put them somewhere people could find. To be of service, in a small way, to my sisters, my pussy posse and maybe even to my besties with testes.

To the daughters, mothers, lovers, friends, co-workers of those women who, due to public disregard and medical neglect, find themselves where I was.

In hormonal exile. In avoidable hell. In the land of the lost.

And what we have lost is balance. Because without hormones, there is no balance, no communication with the body and so many of its primary functions, and without that, comes chaos and mayhem.

We're forgetting, we're sweating. We're aching, we're faking. We're foggy, we're groggy. We're itchy, we're bitchy.

And we're losing; patience, hair, bone density, muscle mass, bladder control, tempers, marriages and jobs.

All because our hard-working hormones have taken indefinite long-service leave — with no intention of ever coming back.

Joni Mitchell once said, "You don't know what you've got 'til it's gone."

I don't think Joni was talking about menopause when she wrote that.

Although I have no doubt that when she went through it herself, she would have seen how perfectly those lyrics applied. Still, even with all that discomfort, we somehow continue to soldier on.

Because we haven't retired, our ovaries have.

We're faking it until we're making it. Depleted and defeated … the show goes on. It's not perfect. Far from it. And neither are we. Because when your body screams sometimes, you do too.

I hope that in my foggy, sweaty, messy odyssey, you will find echoes of your own. And that in some way, this book makes you feel a little less alone.

So, read it straight through. Dip in and out. Pick it up when you need it.

Maybe, it will help you find your own funny.

CONTENTS

I see funny everywhere	vii
Oblivia Newton-John	1
The Inside Job	11
Diary Of A Pre-Teen Pregnancy	26
Peri. Men. Pause.	36
Men Are From Mars And So Is Their Penis	42
Medicine Sans Giving A Shit	47
It's Not A Boy	54
Fani. Not Funny.	59
Sex, Shluck Shlook And The Evil Eye	67
The 34 Symptoms Of Menopause — And Why They're Mostly George's Fault	80
Discovering The Sisterhood	92
Wet T-Shirt Mary	104
The Perfect Pash	112
Be Prepared	124
Apples, Oranges And Dear Dairy	132
The Show Must Go On	141
Seven Percent	152

The Hit And Sit Incident	163
Have Ovaries? Will Menopause	169
Good Thanks	173
The Straight-Talking Guide to Menopause	183
Other Resources	235
Acknowledgments	238
About Mary	240

Menopause
needs a publicist.

We need our besties
to know about it.

We need our
besties with testes
to know about it.

CHAPTER 1

OBLIVIA NEWTON-JOHN

"Silence is golden."

There is supposedly a debate about where that saying comes from and who said it first. (Debate, really?) Winston Churchill famously uttered it. The internet says an erudite guy called Thomas Carlyle first said it back in the ninth century.

Silence as a human virtue. Possibly applicable more to talkative women back then? Maybe old Tom didn't have the poetic balls to say what he really wanted to say,

"Shut up. Keep it to yourself. No one's interested."

Well, Thomas, here's a little heads up, silence is anything but frigging golden when applied to menopause.

Most women suffer in silence when they experience the debilitating symptoms of menopause. Just like I did.

Even after diagnosis, they choose to turn inward rather than 'inflict' their pain on those around them.

I was guilty of doing exactly that.

Silence further promotes the groundless view of menopause as a social stain, rather than a natural state that every woman must face.

Why is it always our first instinct that, no matter what is happening to our bodies, we decide to keep it to ourselves?

Fear of repercussions?

Fear of being wrong?

Fear of being shamed somehow?

In my job, I wear a huge wig, stand up in front of rooms full of people I don't know and routinely tell them exactly what's on my mind (most of it is improvised)

I've been doing that as Effie, my famously fearless character, for over 35 years.

Fear and shame are not things Effie is familiar with.

Fear never made her silent.

Which made my silence all the more uncharacteristic.

Sure, I could legitimately claim that I was hopelessly ignorant because I didn't know enough about menopause. Despite the wealth of material that can be found online, I was blind to it.

So, why didn't I know?

Growing up there were period talks, puberty talks, pregnancy talks, for us teenage girls but no one sat me down and said:

"One day your hormones will riot, your sleep will evaporate, your emotions will burst into flames, and your vagina might start feeling like the Sahara Desert."

Menopause didn't feature in a storyline in any of my favourite TV shows or novels. Nor in any of my Greek aunties' gossip sessions.

It wasn't talked about in my biology class at school or in psychology lectures in university.

I have zero recollection of any proper conversation about it. None. It's like I drank the Kool-Aid of collective amnesia.

There's a collective forgetting that's seeped into our DNA. And I swallowed it whole. But, considering my age, and given there were good friends around me going through it, why didn't I see it coming?

The truth is, I simply didn't rate it. I didn't think it would be significant or a big deal because that's what I'd heard.

And those voices, the ones saying, "it's no biggie" were somehow louder than all the women who, like me, were suffering in silence.

We touched on it in passing over dinner with my girlfriends, but we never delved into it. I wasn't completely oblivious to menopause, but I was totally ignorant of its potential impact on my body and on my life.

I, like way too many, had disregarded menopause as anything truly significant. The sparse stories around it seemed dramatic or over the top and my attitude was that menopause was just another excuse for poor behaviour.

A friend once confessed that she was so full of rage, she threw a frying pan at her husband. I jumped to the conclusion that it must be her mental state not her hormonal state that was the problem. She even told me, "My hormones are driving me crazy. I'm off my rocker." I left that conversation thinking she was, at best, excusing her shitty behaviour and, at worst, laying down a defence for her upcoming homicide trial.

Menopause as an excuse to kill your husband? Please. As if we need one. But I totally get it now.

In the midst of my menopausal maze, I fantasised how my darling and clumsy husband could accidentally fall down the stairs. Oh dear God, why did I have to witness my beloved fall with such force to his untimely death? And what was worse, I was right behind him! So close. Yet so helpless. The guilt was intolerable. Eased only by his life insurance policy.

Then my friend's flying frying pan came to mind. Suddenly I understood. Why was I contemplating killing the man I loved? Who had been my rock through tragedies, triumphs and everything in between for the last twenty years? The answer of course is what's in his pants.

Unlike most men, George is not partial to a bulge in his trousers. I don't know whether it speaks to supreme confidence or just a refusal to buy in to the 'size matters' game, but George has issues with having anything in his pockets that might interfere with his natural shape, like, oh, I don't know, a car key, for example.

Being an advertising man, my dear and way too creative husband often tells me, "I'm an ideas man." As though I'm in the plumbing business and wouldn't understand things like ideas, or thoughts, or notions. George's great idea to combat his bulge-phobia is to separate the car key from the house keys. This is because the car key is considerably bulkier and the main source of any unsightly bulge that may occur. It's a logical course of action, if your only concern is the afore (and often) mentioned bulge, but there is a slight issue.

Keys travel as a group, like the Beatles. Yes, John Lennon can go off and do some wacky stuff with Yoko Ono and Paul

McCartney can go solo, but let's not kid ourselves, they work best when they're together.

"Georgie, I don't mean to get all Nostradamus about it, but I can see a time in the foreseeable future where this leads to serious separation-of-keys anxiety."

This rational concern is often dismissed however, because not being an ideas man, I'm clearly not able to comprehend the elegance of George's thinking. The whole situation is kind of infuriatingly amusing, until it's not.

I had been commissioned by the Sydney Opera House to create and perform a one woman show, "*This Is Personal*" and my director, Blazey Best (and she is) and I were heading to a super important meeting to discuss the technical aspects of the show. While I was busy preparing for the meeting, George dropped our daughter Jamie to school. He got back and as usual, left the car running in the driveway. I jumped in and sped off with just enough time to pick up Blazey on the way.

We were a few minutes from the underground carpark, chatting away, laughing, having a great ol' catch up, when all of a sudden, I looked down at the dashboard and noticed a flashing orange light, 'Car key not in vehicle.' What? Where was the … car… key? Oh, that's right, it was with no bulge George. Do you know that Split Enzymes song, "*I See Red?*" I not only saw red, but also black and blue matching bruises on a guy once known as 'Ideas Man George' who was soon to be remembered as 'Dead Man George'. The police wouldn't need to send out detectives. I would just drive myself, with the key in the car, straight to the police station and happily confess. And I have no doubt whatsoever that if the jury consisted of middle-aged menopausal women I'd get off scot-free. "A clear case of justifiable homicide, your honour."

Google maps calculated the 26-minute round trip for a meeting starting in 9 minutes. As I turned the car around I called him. I needed dead man walking George to be waiting outside, solo key in hand. I was not communicating in any recognisable language. Perplexed, exasperated, I was speaking in scathing, sword-like tongues.

I'm rarely late for meetings. Especially important ones like the one I'm about to be horribly late for, due to his absurd bulge-phobia. I was planning his funeral as I pulled into our street. Ex-husband George was sheepishly waving. I was mentally dictating his eulogy.

When I returned home after the meeting, I let loose such a tsunami of vitriol that stubborn, self-righteous George refused to apologise. He could not understand why my outrage was so over the top and stormed off feeling like he had been hard done by.

He withdrew into his cave. Formulating, as always, a case for an unjustly accused husband.

That night, despite my discomfort and night sweats, which I still attributed to the stress of my forthcoming one woman show, it was very chilly inside our house. *Frozen. The non-musical.* I lay in bed completely baffled by why I had such a huge overreaction. It was so unlike me. What I wish I had known was that hormonally I was running on empty. With my back turned, I listened to snoring, guilty-until-proven-innocent George as I wrestled with how to recover from this ugly episode. And why I went so ballistic.

Next morning I decided to apologise to that absent-minded ideas guy because I felt I went a tad too far with my razor-like tongue. I also wanted him to see that saying sorry is the self-esteem bulge that everyone should aspire to. He might even try it sometime.

My thoughts returned to my frying pan wielding friend. Fury had invaded her veins just like it does for so many of us at the end of our hormonal tether. I understood that first-hand now.

What I didn't understand or feel particularly proud of was that I had so little empathy for what she was going through. That's not at all who I am. Empathy is one of my strong suits. But in that moment it abandoned me and left me incapable of stepping into my friend's shoes. In retrospect, to be honest, there were other moments with other friends where I ignored or dismissed their struggles with menopause due to my complete lack of knowledge.

Two decades ago, one of my pussy posse in her late 30's was having trouble conceiving. She was told by her doctors it was because she was going through early perimenopause.

Did I even clock what that meant back then? I reckon I would have taken more notice if they diagnosed her problem was hairy balls related rather than perimenopause. Back then hairy balls would have been way higher on our conversational agenda. Sad but true.

Another good friend required a full hysterectomy, where both her uterus and ovaries were removed. The operation triggers menopause which causes an immediate drop in estrogen and progesterone. This can lead to abrupt and intense menopause symptoms. In other words, she got an express one-way ticket to hormonal Hellsville. And my response? Well, dumb, ignorant, knows nothing Mary, from memory sent a fruit basket. Good one me.

The embarrassing recollections are flooding back. A girlfriend and I were sharing a hotel room when I spotted her wearing what I now realise was an MHT patch. Did I ask, "Hey what's with the sticker, sister?" Nope. But I guarantee that if she had a new pair of Jimmy Choo's on, I would have been all over those.

If I'd listened more intently every time something like that came up, I might have been a better friend. I may have been more supportive. I would have connected my own mystifying menopausal dots sooner and avoided some of that unnecessary pain. I know I'm not the only woman who underestimated and dismissed menopause in that way. Since then I've heard other women confess their own judgmental blind spots. And their own fraught and punishing journeys. Sadly, it's an all too common road. But still, that's not good enough.

They say knowledge is power. Yet at the peak of my power as a woman, my ignorance rendered me powerless. There are gaps in knowledge. And gaps in logic. There are gendered biases that even affect our view of our own gender. It's complex, complicated and convoluted — which is three ways of saying it seems too conspiratorial, not only from the outside but from the inside too. It's a medical, male/female, social conundrum that needs to be addressed and unravelled. It's a mystery we need to expose and do more about.

It's an enigma not a stigma. Menopause needs a publicist. We need our besties to know all about it. We need our besties with testes to know more about it. We need our doctors to know a lot more about it. We need our workplaces to talk about it. How many millions of women over the years were casualties of menopausal medical misdiagnosis?

What we do know is that things can change. And they must. Most of all, we do not want our daughters unprepared and uninformed. When menopause happened to me, I didn't seek any help or discuss it with anyone. How could I when I didn't even recognise it?

All I knew was that something was happening to me and I chose to go it alone. As a so-called aware, educated, middle-aged woman, I should have known more about fleeing hormones and the rampant emotional and physical upheavals they would create.

But I was clueless. Completely in the dark.

I was Oblivia Newton-John.

My daily rage urges had accumulated enough frequent-fury points to get me Platinum status.

Unfortunately, there are no benefits.

CHAPTER 2

THE INSIDE JOB

For me, menopause initially felt like being in one of those bleak TV mystery series full of brilliant British actors with amazing range and bad teeth. There's been a murder, and things look grim. The case seems impossible to solve.

Let's set the scene:

The outline of a hormonally abandoned body is found at the scene of the crime.

There were no eyewitnesses to come forward to shed light on this tragedy and help with the inquiry. Just an all-pervasive sense of something very evil bubbling under the surface.

There are no clues, except for one — the consensus among those closest to her that, for some time, the victim had not been "herself." Not much of a clue, given that the victim was a professional actress and had spent a lifetime getting paid to *not* be "herself."

Delving deeper, we discover that, privately, this usually well-informed actress was losing herself and morphing into someone she could barely recognise.

And while she was used to doing so, having, throughout her career played a hairdresser, a policewoman, a lawyer, a therapist, a judge, a man, a child and even a dog, this time it was different. For a start, she wasn't getting paid.

In fact, this new 'role' was costing her plenty, her ability to reason, her sleep and even her sanity.

Trying to solve this endocrinological enigma was like trying to align the matching squares of a psychological Rubik's cube, and there was not a brilliant nimble-fingered Asian boy in sight to solve the puzzle.

There were plenty of clues and DNA evidence, but the murder weapon was nowhere to be found.

Like most women discomfort and pain were things I was quite familiar with thanks to puberty, multiple IVF's, miscarriages, a still-born baby, still more IVF's, another pregnancy, a birth, recovery from pregnancy, etc. Granted, nothing as serious as man flu or erectile dysfunction, but nevertheless, I'd seen my share of both mental and physical difficulties.

With any previous distress or discomfort, I was quick to outsource my struggles to experts. The things I knew I couldn't solve on my own, were the domain of professionals who knew better, who could help.

The one role I knew I never wanted to play was "Mary the Martyr" yet, this time, the idea of reaching out to someone to help me find the source of my misery didn't even seem like an option.

This time, for some dumb reason, I felt I had to deal with this mysterious malady myself.

At the time, this made perfect sense to me. After all, who better to solve the 'crime' than a clueless, poorly-equipped detective who had compromised skin in the game, right? Exactly.

Immediately, I set off on the wrong path.

Instead of trying to work out what was happening to me at that exact moment, I decided that maybe a more effective course of action would be to look at what had already happened to me in the past and the things with which I'd been dealing with in the long term to see if there were any clues there.

Maybe I would uncover some underlying pattern by diving into the past. So began the painstaking process of elimination in which I probed the prime suspects.

Was it grief? I have had considerable experience with this suspect, and I don't recommend it. Unfortunately, it's been something of a constant in my life. If you dare to love, then it's the price you pay, again and again. However, when something is so constant, we do tend to learn to live with it.

Was it depression? That old despair-filled chestnut. I'm also quite familiar with that one. Though it doesn't come naturally to me, when you run out of hope, it can lead you to some dark places. Luckily, I'd surrounded myself with incredibly dedicated professional and non-professional sherpas (yes, the ones I was now ignoring) who guided me from the scary abyss in which I'd found myself and guided me back on track.

Was it anxiety? The hyper-active, high-pitched, ugly sister of worry. No-one needs to listen to that focus-pulling, nagging, negative Narelle. Best to shut that wingeing bitch down ASAP.

Was it stress? Or as I like to call it: excitement's nemesis. A handbrake to all healthy things. Overused and overrated. I don't know whose publicist stress is, but they need to be sacked, packed and racked, right off.

Okay, so those were all the 'emotional' suspects, and while there seemed to be elements of them in what I was feeling, none quite fit the bill perfectly enough for them to be the main offender.

What about some of the outsiders, the external things that were going on around me, could they be the cause of my malaise?

For example, there was a little thing going on at the time called a global pandemic. Talk about next level madness. COVID-19 felt like the entire world was going through menopause. It certainly contributed to the re-emergence of some previously identified suspects, but we got through it. It was soon over, so it couldn't be them.

Was it world politics? Honestly, it's hard not to lose faith in humanity when the price of winning is at the cost of it. When some fake tan and some fake news can bring the entire planet to such a state of misery, there doesn't seem to be much reason for hope.

Was it my poor dying dog? Imagine the cutest, love-filled bundle of joy fading before your eyes. The devastating, soul-crushing heartbreak of watching my adorable nappy-wearing companion of 16 years struggle to stand up or eat. Torture.

Was it my beautiful, courageous, inspiring daughter? Brighter than a star, cuter than a nappy-wearing dog and surprisingly, given her abundance of talents, seemingly a lot less resourceful.

Anyone who has heard the phrase, "Mumma could you…?" and been asked to do something you know can be achieved without you, can identify with this one.

"Mumma could you…?" still triggers the following internal monologue, "I could. But couldn't you? I think you should. Does that mean you would? Because I know you could." A promising little suspect here.

But then again, so was my beautiful, baffled, beleaguered beau, George. Struggling with issues of his own, his constant, "What's up with you Mou?" became annoying. Bordering on infuriating.

'Mou' is his affectionate nickname for me. It means 'mine' in Greek. It also happens to be the noise a cow makes so it's one of those words that you judge according to context and tone of the user.

George made it clear that he had noticed a change in me, that I was not my 'usual' self, that something was 'up'.

Could that something be him? Or maybe something that he'd done? I didn't want to blame George, but if you were to ask me at the time, I'd say the chances were very high that my torment could be laid squarely at his broad Greek feet. He was my obvious target. Who else could press my buttons so effortlessly? Menopause had engineered the perfect decoy to hide behind. The husband.

Anything he did, had done or was doing was sufficient circumstantial evidence for a conviction.

They say the main suspect always returns to the scene of the crime, and given that George was working from home, he never seemed to leave the scene. He himself would openly admit that, at times, he had the motive to commit the crime, given my increasingly erratic behaviour. But then again, I had plenty of motives to commit some crimes myself — his snoring, his chewing (often of liquids), his obliviousness. I could go on, but I won't (well, I will, a lot, but that's later).

To be completely honest, there were days, and plenty of them, where George, suspect number one, and my cute user daughter with her relentless "Can you do this for me?" and "Can you get that for me?" were really pushing their luck.

Those were the 'watch your back because I'd had enough' days. I'd had enough of covering backs. Big ones, small ones, hers and his ones. Especially when nobody seemed to be covering mine. Not only did they need to watch their backs, they also needed to watch their fronts and their sides too.

The daily rage urges had accumulated enough frequent-fury points to get me Platinum status. Unfortunately, that loyalty program comes with no benefits.

My already severely eroded patience was running out and under the surface of my barely-holding-on veneer, wrath was bubbling. I was on the brink of exploding like a human Mount Etna.

Regularly, small and medium-sized outbursts would sneak out of me, like accidental farts. My volume would suddenly peak without warning. My stone-faced, Botox-style expressions would momentarily stop them in their tracks. But not for long. In their minds I must have had a persistent case of the Gladys Knight and The Pips.

I stopped living in share households when I left university because I like living in tidy and beautiful environments.

And I stopped being a housemaid at the Hilton when I was twenty-one because I got sick of cleaning up after people all day long.

So, when someone doesn't put things away or does only half a job, leaving the other half for us to do, or doesn't think to set the table when you've cooked a great meal, it makes me feel like I'm 'house sharing housemaid Mary'.

I'm good with doing a lot. I'm like my mother. I'm lucky that I was born with great energy. I love getting things done. But at the same time it doesn't mean I like doing everything.

George is a gentleman. He's not old fashioned. He's a grown up and he can take care of himself. And he's not lazy. But he's busy. And so am I.

Does he care if I cook? Probably not. He can cook too.

Do I cook? Yes. Does he cook? Yes. Do I cook more? Probably.

Does he expect me to put the washing on? Probably not. He can put the washing on. Do I put the washing on more? Probably.

Do I do food shopping? Yes. Does he do food shopping? Yes. Do I do more? Probably.

George is very easy to live with. I think it's because he moved out of home at a young age like I did. So, he's very self-sufficient.

He's clean, yes. He's tidy, yes. But he loves to engage the services of multiples. It's never one pair of socks on the go, no. It's "These socks are only for walking, these socks are for working and these socks are for hanging out." That's three pairs of socks or six singular socks that are hanging around somewhere not too far away. Then there's "The working gear, the walking gear and the hanging out gear." All these items are in waiting. Then there's "The hats in summer and the beanies in winter."

All these useful regularly used items need somewhere to rest. So, I get hooks. Many, many good-looking wooden hooks to hang these things from, so that they are not on chairs or in bathrooms or spreading themselves in places that they shouldn't spread themselves. But somehow no matter how many hooks a girl can offer a man with many things to hang, there's never quite enough.

And boy does he love a glass jar. He does. Nowhere near as much as his mother loves a plastic bag, but if you don't challenge him those jars multiply.

The reason, "It could be good for something"

"Yes, recycling, that's what it's good for."

Thankfully, he's not into punnets. But his parents are. To my in-laws punnets are like puppies. They never met a punnet they didn't want to keep. And don't get me started on the amount of tissue boxes at my in-laws' house. They're everywhere. You don't even need to fully extend your arm and "Wham, there's a tissue box."

I borrowed my father in-law's car recently and there was a family sized tissue box the size of the commission flats smack in the middle of the dash. I could barely see out the windscreen. How that tissue box doesn't slide across from right to left every time he turns a corner is a complete mystery. If it does slide in the wrong direction and you are desperately in need of a tissue, do not panic because there are more tissues in the side doors, as well as a box in the back seat.

The need for multiples is definitely in George's family DNA.

A bit like the former Chinese one child policy, I'm pro the one pair of socks and the one tissue box policy. It's logical and less to tidy and that matters to a neat freak like me.

My daughter is gorgeous, cute and unless told, she will not put things away. She says she will, but does she? Why put it away when Mumma could put it away?

Well, the honest answer to that is, "Mumma, is sick of putting things away! In fact, she's sick of buying things, washing things, cooking things, hanging things and saying things."

Don't get me wrong. My family are good people. They say, "Thank you" and "I love you" and "You're the best." And I love that they do that. But maybe we need a few less "I love yous" and a few more "How are you?" Or "Can I help you?"

Is that so hard? Especially when you know I've barely slept thanks to that bastard called, you guessed, it menopause and I'm wrecked.

"Mumma are you poopy?"

"Yes, amongst other things."

George: "Maybe you should go out for a walk."

Suddenly we agree.

Me: "Maybe getting out's a good idea."

"Don't be gone too long, Mumma, I'll miss you."

"Dada can get you anything you want Monkey."

George: "Actually, I've got a zoom in 15."

Me: "Like I said, DADA can get you anything you want!!"

And out I would walk.

Sadly, because of the lockdowns I couldn't, in the words of the Gladys Knight song, catch the midnight train to Georgia, as neither of the Georgia's were within a five-kilometre radius.

On those walks, I would take the opportunity to once again trawl through my suspect list and I would either calm down or be overcome by a tsunami of anxiety. During those times, my thought process would go as follows;

I knew that I was being affected by not being able to work or see my friends — my chosen family, my oxygen, the most uncomplicated part of my emotional life. We get and give the best of ourselves to each other. We cry, we buy, we laugh, we barf, we talk, we walk. We have decades of shared memories, conversations, celebrations and devastations. We know each other's histories, families and children. We were young with very little and yet created so much — careers, babies, homes. And while much was lost, there were gains many, many, gains.

But then COVID winded the world, separating us from our greatest resource: each other. The price we paid was huge.

Yes, there were moments, even in that crazy wild time, that were good. But nowhere near enough to heal the scars of separation.

The new normal wasn't the sanitising or mask wearing — it was living life in fear and solitude. The pandemic sent a simple message to the world and that was — no one is safe.

Going through undiagnosed menopause during that time was excruciatingly difficult because not only was the world telling us that everything had changed but my body was telling me too. Not that I fully understood. Whatever it was amplified my anxiety, my dread, my inability to rest. And it diminished my hope.

My humour didn't die, but it was definitely in remission.

I tried to decipher what was happening to me it but I couldn't, the fog was too thick.

So, I did what I often do when I find myself somewhere difficult, I try to write myself out of it. And where better to put all these feelings than on the page? That's when Effie's new stage show, *Better Out Than In* was born. Effie spoke about the punishment of lockdowns and comically vomited up all the COVID emotions, frustrations and hysteria.

"At the beginning I was like, Corona? Relax will ya's what's the big deal? Within 48 hours my paranoia had red-lined. When it came to sanitising, I was like Sara Lee, layer upon layer upon layer. And masks? One was never enough. To be extra safe I had to do two, like a double condom."

Effie spoke about writing a COVID memoir called, 'Eat, Pray, Eat' and having to home school her little boofy daughter which was torture.

"My little pride and joy, Aphie (Aphrodite) is now primary school age which tragically for her means she had to rely on me to home school her. I've been called a lot of things in my life, but 'scholastic' is not one of them. You can imagine how guilty I felt putting my child's intellectual future into my Instagram addicted hairdresser hands."

Meanwhile, when I wasn't writing jokes I was back in the reality of my menopausal life. Stuck at home day after day with a kid that needed home-schooling and a husband that needed 'How not to give me the pips' schooling was wearing. No doubt, that combined with all those other suspects, aided and abetted what I was feeling.

But still I had the nagging feeling that it was bigger than all of that.

It was as though each of those factors had been injected with some kind of super-steroid. It was psychological, no doubt, but it was physical too. It was heavy. A load I could barely carry. Like the weight of the world was upon me.

When I slept, or tried to, it woke me up, refusing to let me rest. When I lay down it tried to keep me there, as though I was stuck to my bed by a massive king-sized magnet. The only way to get out of bed was to slowly slide out of it. Even breathing was arduous, as though every emotion was trying to release itself with each breath from my compressed and constricted chest.

And yet I was silent. I battled with it in my brain. Internalising it. Hoping that it would somehow diminish. Or even better, disappear, never to return. But it didn't. It didn't because it couldn't. And it couldn't because it was trapped.

Trapped in me.

That's when I came to the painful realisation that this had nothing to do with a painful past or a present that seemed perennially on pause.

This was not about grief or Jamie or George. Prior to this conclusion George was definitely the prime suspect and Jamie a person of interest, but that was no longer the case.

The more evidence I was accumulating the more it pointed to the fact that those two loveable and frequent wrongdoers were no longer under investigation. The evidence was conclusive. The one-person jury had reached its verdict. The suspect was under my roof the whole time. They were under my nose, literally. That guilty party, that suspect was me!

Me? Of all people, me.

Yes, it was an inside job.

But now that I had solved the case, I knew that all I needed was someone, anyone, to help me deal with the horrendous hormonal heist that had taken place.

All that was left now was to take the usual action, outsource the problem, find an expert, get some advice or some treatment and bring the culprit to justice.

Simple, right?

Not really.

As I began my search for someone to help me, I realised that the real mystery had only begun. Let's put it this way, I don't know how rare hen's teeth are but given what I was experiencing trying to get advice, doctors who are trained in dealing with menopause are even rarer.

What. Are. You. Talking. About. Willis?

I was astonished, which is a nice Anglo-suburban way of saying how pissed off I was.

I was facing a life-changing event that every woman will face in her life, and I could not find anyone who had specific expertise in it? Why?

(See my previous question to Willis.)

The answer hit me before the question even got out. Why was there no one I could find to help me with such a common issue for women?

That's right, because it only happens to women.

And when I look back, this is always how it had happened to me where my body was involved. I would feel things happening and I'd dismiss them.

I mean, what's a bit of pain or discomfort when there is fun to be had, or work to do, or obligations to fulfil?

Then, something would happen, an eruption, an excretion, an explosion, some other 'e' thing. Cue panic and suffering, cries for help, a band aid solution and back to life — fun, work, obligations.

It's how most women live their lives, prioritising what they want and what's expected of them over their physical needs. It's as though we are locked in a constant battle with our bodies, a battle that we think we are winning. We don't realise that for every eruption, there's a disruption, for every excretion, there's a deletion, for every explosion there's…

Okay, I can't think of anything, but you get my point.

In a game of rock, paper, scissors, the body always wins.

It's better to be known as the kid who shat her pants than the kid whose body was doing slippery, tingly things.

CHAPTER 3

DIARY OF A PRE-TEEN PREGNANCY

"Where ignorance is bliss, 'tis folly to be wise."

A poet called Thomas Gray wrote that in 1742, which makes it two old white guys named Thomas with bad advice so far. (And the first of two Grays, but I'll get into that in *"Men Are From Mars And So Is Their Penis"*.)

It's the same idea as "what you don't know, can't hurt you", and if you've ever woken in the middle of the night feeling like someone has set you on fire or tried walking around when it feels like your underwear is made of sandpaper, you know the old white guys got it wrong again.

While it's true that ignorance is the main reason I was late to the menopause 'party' — and I'm usually the first to arrive at any party — it's also true that I do have a history of ignoring what's going on in my body, especially when there are other priorities that are more pressing, or more fun.

I'm not only usually the first to arrive, I'm also always the last to leave, and I ignore my body's warnings and keep going. Of course, I've paid for it on numerous occasions, but the cost was never as heavy as the one I experienced when my hormones fled for pastures new.

The first instance I can remember of ignoring my body's warning signs occurred when I was five years old. I was at my friend's house, next door to ours, with her, her brother and a bunch of other kids from the neighbourhood. I can't even remember what we were doing, but I have the very strong impression that I was having the best time ever.

Then I felt the first rumble. I knew what it meant, of course. And even though I was sitting on the step and leaning against the toilet door (which was part of the undercover patio area), I still chose to ignore my bowel's call. Plus, the door handle was too high for me to reach.

"Don't worry about it," My five-year-old brain told me. "Just relax and have fun."

So, I did. Then the next rumble happened. And while I tried to stay focused on the fun, I went into deep, intense negotiation with my body.

"Mary, it's your bum. You've gotta do something!"

"Hey, don't tell me what to do, all right? I'm having fun."

"Mary, listen, things are about to get ugly. And you don't want that 'ugly' to happen in front of everyone. Why don't you just…"

"Hey, I'm the boss. Not my bum. Give me some time!"

And that's when time ran out.

As full as my heart was with joy, it paled in comparison to how full my undies suddenly got. I froze for a few seconds, not really sure what I should do. When you're five, you're not overly blessed with resources for handling awkward social situations. But when the fun and play continued, I became convinced that I had gotten away with it. That's when my friend's brother Peter raised a finger in the air as a signal for us to stop, and everybody instantly became motionless. Like a zebra sensing a subtle shift on the savannah, his nostrils flared as he sniffed the air. "Errrr! I smell shit!" Oh, nooooo..."Who did a shit?"

I sat with an innocent blank, 'well it's obviously not me' expression on my face while the steamy, stinky evidence was brewing downstairs. He instantly morphed from zebra to bloodhound as he walked amongst us, leaning in with his pronounced Greek nose, trying to isolate the source of the smell. Panic had now set in: "Please God, no please… don't say it."

Then his finger pointed at no-longer-innocent little Mary: "It's you! You shit your pants!"

I fled.

Crying, I ran next door screaming, "Mama, Mama." Sobbing with humiliation and with a river of snot dangling from my bright red nose, I told the story to my mother.

To her credit, she saw the degree of my upset and didn't bother to institute the usual standard Greek protocols. Which, typically when I did something wrong, was an introduction to the 'five brothers', otherwise known as a slap. Instead, she went straight into rigorous evidence-eradicating action by whisking away the reeking mound of muck, meticulously cleaning me up and promptly providing some fresh undies and clothes.

As I sat there, sniffling, ashamed and grateful, I reflected on what had happened. My body hadn't really betrayed me; I just hadn't listened hard enough, and now I was faced with a massive humiliation that would stay with me forever. Or at least three minutes, after which I decided everything was fine, and went straight back to my friend's place and got back to the fun and games.

You have a certain social and scatological resilience when you're five, but I was determined that from now on, me and my body would be on the same wavelength.

So, it's three years later. Same house, same friend, and we're seated in front of the TV watching the matinee movie. Once again, I have no memory of what the movie was. All I can be certain of is that it was some kind of romance, that it was black and white, and we were totally getting into it. I loved love. Getting crushes was one of my favourite things to get, other than a Cadbury Flake or a new pair of white Levi jeans.

At eight years old, both my friend and I were becoming conscious of, well, you can't really call it sex, so let's call it the intersectionality of girls and boys. We knew that, at some point in the future, this intersectionality might be something that would seem desirable or appeal to us. Maybe it's the reason we chose to watch a romance, even though Abbot and Costello were on the other channel running away from ghosts, or werewolves, or mummies on a boat, or in a haunted castle, or in the jungle or something. I don't remember any of the details of the plot or who was in the movie. The one image I do remember is that right near the end, with the music swelling dramatically, the couple in the movie lock into an intense kiss, after which they open a door and walk through. Fade. The End.

That's when my body did something I had never experienced before. This time it wasn't a rumble. It was something else, something totally new. It started in my girlie bits and spread everywhere. It was like a tingling, ticklish Mexican wave that took over my whole body. Having learned my lesson three years before, without any hesitation, I immediately fled the scene.

I was out of there and in my bathroom with the door locked in less than forty-five seconds. I didn't know what was going on, but I knew something major had just happened. I grabbed some toilet paper to wipe myself and it was so slick and slippery that when I wiped 'down there' I nearly dislocated my shoulder. I felt like Dennis Lillee, the famous Australian fast bowler. If you've ever watched cricket, I think you get the visual. What just happened?? My mind raced, trying to make sense of something I couldn't make sense of.

It could only be one thing: I must be pregnant.

I sat on the toilet seat bereft of other possibilities, crying and clutching my thighs, and rocking backwards and forwards. I had stolen the rocking backwards and forwards bit from one of my favourite movies at the time, *Change Of Habit*, starring Elvis Presley and Mary Tyler Moore. Elvis played a doctor in a ghetto clinic who falls in love with a nun played by Mary, who, because her convent is one of those ultra-hip 1960s kind of convents, is dressed in normal street clothes and not a habit (hence the pun, get it?). So, you can understand Elvis' confusion.

In the movie, there was a young, non-verbal autistic girl called Amanda who rocked backwards and forwards when she was stressed and who had hot Dr Elvis and sweet nun

Mary Tyler Moore try to heal her love. It's intense, dramatic and has some great songs that, like in all Elvis movies, come organically from the drama and aren't just bolted on (okay, I'm lying, they were bolted on like a loose rusty muffler).

In my little bathroom drama, I added tears to the rocking back and forth as a way of dealing with the pressure of a parental predicament I had never imagined finding myself in as an 8-year-old. Plus, I think I was dipping my toe into acting by rehearsing the most dramatic, or in this case, melodramatic, scene possible.

How was I going to tell my parents that they would soon be grandparents? How do you raise a baby without a job, and what job was I even qualified for? And what was I going to call her? It felt like a "her". Natasha maybe? Natasha is such a great name for a girl. It sounds so posh. Or maybe Amanda, like the girl in *Change of Habit*. I loved the name Amanda because you can shorten it to Mandy; for most of my life I wanted to be a Mandy because it was close to Mary but way cooler. What if it was a boy? Brandon or Brett could work. Although maybe my parents/the grandparents would want a Greek name.

So many decisions and responsibilities. The baby wasn't even born yet, and already there were so many pressures.

There I was, eight years old, somehow knowing but not knowing that I had just had my first ever orgasm, even though I hadn't even heard the word or knew of the concept, convinced that my life was over, picking baby names.

It was heart-breaking, world-shattering anguish and it stayed with me — for about two minutes — until my brother, Con, knocked on the bathroom door. "Hey, we're going to play footy. You wanna join?" Footy?! Absolutely!

By the time we were at the park, playing kick to kick, I'd forgotten I was ever 'with child'. The image of a life in poverty raising little Mandy or Brandon or Theo or Spiro or Eleni or even baby Effie was quickly fading from my mind. Once again, I had avoided any consequences to do with my bodily functions.

In retrospect (or 'Googlespect', which is the online version of retrospect) I know that this was probably a sign of something referred to as 'peri-puberty' (yep, I'm learning about a lot of 'the peris' way too late) which is a time leading up to the first stages of puberty and can occur in girls as young as eight and in boys as young as nine. It's a time when the hormones are just moving in. They may not have unpacked all the boxes, set up the sound system and flat screen yet, but they have definitely set up the kitchen and started cooking away. Or maybe it wasn't. I don't really know, because I didn't mention it to anyone until I was way into my adulthood.

Because that's what you did. You didn't talk about these things.

A practice that would see me completely floored by menopause later in life. The only lessons I took away from the whole thing was that it's better to be known as the kid who shat her pants than the kid whose body was doing slippery, tingly things. That became my pattern, my logic, my strategy, and I don't think I'm alone in this.

As women, we expose the parts of ourselves we're comfortable with. Anything that makes us look bad, we bury. We pretend those parts don't exist and hope they just go away if we ignore them long enough. And then there are the bits we don't understand, the mysterious parts of being human. The parts we fear. The parts that could be clues to something we don't really want to investigate in case they are incriminating or, even worse, sinister.

So, we sit in ignorance, fear and discomfort. Because, as women, we're accustomed to that. And we wait for clarity to fall out of the sky, or the internet, or hope for a random slap-in-the-face conversation to enlighten us. To lighten the load of womanhood. And the load is heavy sometimes.

It's there in both superficial and substantial ways. It's there every time we walk to our cars with our fearful, fast beating hearts late at night.

It's there when hair grows in places where we would rather it didn't.

It's there when our bodies become beacons of attention we don't need or want.

It's there every month for a week when wearing white is not an option.

It's there in the tone and actions of people we loved and thought were trustworthy.

It's there when we compare ourselves to others.

It's there when the world is telling us we are not enough.

It's there when we have dreams that appear a million miles away.

It's there when we forget to love ourselves well.

It's there at every scan, every blood test, and every pap smear.

It's there, always.

And it doesn't go away. But it can fade. And it can be argued with and won. It can be a teacher, a bodyguard, and a lesson learnt. And it can be a reminder that good people, good information, and a good sense of humour are there to ease those crushing moments of what being human means. I try to twist those awkward, often heartbreaking, moments into entertaining, useful assets after the pain begins to subside.

I try to find the funny.

But there's an intrinsic contradiction between what the body wants slash needs and what the mind and heart want that women face every day but men don't really have to, which doesn't sit well with me and never has.

How is it, for example, that women are born with a finite number of eggs, whereas men are still cranking out the sperm, willy-nilly-Nelson, like a productive sperm making assembly line well into their 80's? Hello? Robert DeNiro, Al Pacino and Mick Jagger?

How is it, that for so many women, one minor problem can lead to massive complications when trying to conceive, while you need to surgically sever some vital plumbing (well, pretty much the only plumbing) to get men to even stop? Hello, gendered genital reproductive bias.

I love to find the funny, but whose idea of a joke is that?

Menopause is a change in seasons – a physical weather event.

Sadly, a lot of doctors are terrible meteorologists.

CHAPTER 4

PERI. MEN. PAUSE.

Perimenopause is the body's equivalent of a flight attendant's safety demonstration: painful but extremely necessary.

The sudden mood swings, irregular periods, hot flashes and, my favourite, "urinary emergencies" you experience in perimenopause are all indicators of the hormonal crash that's coming. A sign that you need to take steps like putting on your life jacket, checking your drop-down oxygen mask and getting into the brace position. You're still going to hit the side of the mountain and go up in a fiery ball of destruction, but hey, at least you know it's on the way.

Without doubt, one of the main reasons that menopause hit me so hard was that, in my forties, a time when most women face perimenopause, I was going through one fertility treatment after another: 23 IVFs in total, in my quest to have a child.

I have written extensively about my IVF 'journey' before, so let's just say it was epic and try to keep it short.

Though I had always wanted a child, I didn't want to be married until I met George. Though I was well into my thirties, that body clock that I'd heard about hadn't ever really got my attention, but with my record, I don't know whether I just wasn't listening. Then meeting George got all the alarms ringing at once.

I knew I wanted to marry George on our first date, despite his propensity to ask rhetorical questions which he would then answer himself. Which was okay, because I enjoyed listening to him. He was entertaining and intelligent and grounded. I'm not sure when it was, maybe between rhetorical questions five and six, that this thought occurred to me: "George is the first man I've ever dated." Until then, I had only ever dated boys.

A little while later, I met his gorgeous five-year-old son, Tom Tom, and fell in love all over again.

My father had many insights that I carry to this day, but his greatest joy were things that made life a little easier. Whenever we would lose him at a shopping centre, all we had to do to track him down was find where the latest household gadget was being demonstrated. He was fascinated by anything that seemed innovative or convenient.

Carpet tiles were his favourite: "You spill a drink, it doesn't matter, just lift the tile and swap it for one from under the couch."

His love of convenience extended to 'matters of the heart' as well. When one of my brother's friends married a woman with two children, he was really impressed: "How smart is Mark? He's got an instant family. Genius!"

That's how I felt about George and Tom Tom. They were my instant family, and I wanted nothing more than to grow that family, but soon after we got married, I was told that it would be almost impossible for me to have a child. I may not have been very good at listening to my body, but I heard that loud and clear, and the key word I heard was 'almost'.

Long story long, it took almost a decade, took us to the other side of the world, to Athens, to try there with a brilliant Greek-Australian doctor called Dr Kon Pantos (otherwise known as The Pelican due to his remarkable success rate). And that's where I finally fell pregnant.

The cast and crew included: Family, Friends, Fertility Doctors, Midwives, Nurses, Egg Donors, Priests, Chiropractors, Colonic Irrigationists, the Waiters, Cooks and Suppliers at Thanassi's Kebabery in Athens, and at least one Egyptian Fortune Teller.

So, even if I was due to experience menopause at that age, because of the number of hormones and other things too numerous to list being injected into my system, its symptoms were either hidden or arrested. I didn't get the chance to even put on the life jacket. All I got was the loud explosion and sudden crash.

I've come to see menopause as a change in seasons — a physical weather event. Sadly, a lot of doctors are terrible meteorologists. I had incredible trouble finding one that even noticed the change in weather, let alone was able to predict it.

For some, menopause might be a little bit of flash flooding for others it's a huge deluge. Some suffer through heatwaves, others through periods of extreme drought — mostly in the southern regions. Extreme conditions make for extreme emotions. And that can be extremely costly. And if you're not careful, your hormones might not be the only thing you lose.

Many marriages are lost during menopause, and it can become the straw that breaks the married camel's back.

Women feel taken for granted and unsupported, and men feel blamed and unloved. You think back to how your marriage started. You remember that day vividly as one of the happiest days of your life. You stood there fully committed, and you made a vow: "For better or worse, in sickness and in health, till death of hormones hopefully do not do us part."

And yet there you are decades later, contemplating murder. How did it get to this? Who is this person I'm with? Why do they look so familiar? And why does this person use every utensil in the kitchen when they cook and spread their mess like a virus across every surface?

It seems some things are invisible, and others are not. He fails to see the kitchen mess or the outdoor plants that need watering, but if Scarlett Johansson was five hundred meters away in a G-string, I'm sure he could describe every curvy detail and the pertness of each cheek. Maybe there really is such a thing as gendered selective seeing...

The phrase men are visual creatures is a common one. Evolutionary psychologists believe it's linked to mate selection. Unsurprisingly, it does not seem anywhere near as efficient during chore selection. Men are very good at seeing what they like. The partnership between their eyes, brain and penis is a fascinating one. A bit like the Bermuda Triangle it too is known for unusual activity, natural phenomena and much human error. It is not uncommon for things to go missing in this region: concentration, logic, and willpower. Ultimately, the compass in their pants, the magnetic needle, that points due north is what helps determine the direction they take. And boy, that needle really loves to point north.

Domestic data, however, has been collected by females which proves that a sink full of dishes or a full laundry basket immediately turns that needle 180 degrees due south.

The differences between women and men are endless, but plenty of us still choose to commit a lifetime to trying to make sense of them all.

To his credit, George did notice the changes in me, even before I did. Always a keen monitor of biorhythms, he became aware of an imbalance and, after eliminating all possible suspects, like my glands, his glands and just glands in general, he was super committed to helping me discover what was going on.

Without George, I don't think I would have reached the conclusion that I was going through menopause so quickly. He was super supportive and did everything he could to get as informed as I was about menopause. Then he made the mistake all men make.

He tried to fix it.

I'm forever grateful
to be a woman.

I knew that 1000%
the first time
I saw a penis.

CHAPTER 5

MEN ARE FROM MARS AND SO IS THEIR PENIS

According to the John Gray book, '*Men are from Mars and Women are from Venus*, men are very solution focused. They love to fix problems immediately, whereas women seek connection by being heard and understood. There might be some truth in that. My issue with the way John puts it is it makes women sound onerous and wearing, while males sound like capable action men. I beg to differ with John. Actually, I don't beg. I just differ.

From what I have witnessed, those capable action men can't remember to jump into action on a very high percentage of things that need doing. Just sayin', John.

Gray also states that "the secret to empowering a man is to never try to change him or improve him." John, now that is a guy's name, right? So, and I'm just guessing here, maybe it suits him to say that. And, just quietly, women love nothing more than to renovate a man. It's a bit like a property. Over time, you need to do a bit of sprucing, it's the only way to get a decent return on investment.

I'm sorry, but my argument is simple — if guys feel the need to provide immediate solutions to women's problems, then women need to provide immediate solutions to theirs. Example: locking the front door when men are wearing oversized cargo shorts, calf length black socks and ugly runners. That sounds fair, doesn't it, John?

We all have our blind spots. And it's healthy to choose to love people that can open our eyes to them.

Not that my husband, George, could have done that for me when I was lost in the wilderness of menopause. That was a 'me' thing to do. Actually, a 'we' thing. A 'we women' thing. And we need to do more. We need to talk about it more. Prepare for it more. Not be so blindsided by it all. I found out the hard way. The way too hard way. But I know more now than I did before.

There's plenty that we, as women, go through. Would I want to be a man? No. Although I did have a dream once that I had a penis, and I have to confess it felt unbelievable, but not incredible enough for me to want to walk around with that swinging, distracting, odd-looking pendulum between my legs. Again, no thank you.

I love being a woman too much.

I love what our bodies are capable of.

I love our intuition.

I love our empathy.

I love that we are soft.

I love that we are strong.

I love that we bring balance and beauty to the world.

I love having front row seats to the sensation of human creation.

I love the fashion.

I love the passion.

Over time, we have worked out what matters and what doesn't. And we realise we are defined by our personal experience, not by the world's unrealistic ideals. I know how much currency youthfulness holds. But like all shiny new things, it depreciates over time.

So, I invest in the things that don't: in experiences. In capacities. In talents. In relationships. In friendships. In community. And by doing that, I am investing in secure evergreen stocks that are guaranteed to deliver, like gold.

There's beauty in ageing. There's comfort in wisdom. And there's peace in gratitude. As women, we forever wear our hearts on our sleeves. And our history on our faces. We come into the world looking like perfectly ironed cotton shirts, only to, decades later, look like creased linen ones. Luckily, I prefer linen. Okay, I confess, after a bad night's sleep or in the wrong lighting, I wouldn't be opposed to a significant steam-pressed ironing and a substantial spritzing of Fabulon.

I think one of the most challenging aspects of getting older, though, is losing our relevance. We have to fight to maintain that. I also think that we give too much power to others instead of investing in our own. But when it comes to our medical issues, most of us endow doctors with having the answers because we are vulnerable and afraid.

So, no, I would never want to be a man, with their selective vision and pendulums getting caught in their zippers. Or their regular genital hydraulic issues. Despite all we endure, I would rather be a woman… unless it comes to health matters, where things seem to be ever so slightly skewed toward the male. But they do endure so much more than us.

We all remember that devastating global erectile dysfunction emergency, don't we?

Thank God for all those heroic, dedicated people in the pharmaceutical profession who laboured tirelessly to solve that one.

Everything's tougher for men. Even the IVF process. All women have to do is consent to a physically and psychologically devastating routine that leaves us feeling like a cross between human pincushions and crash-test dummies. In the meantime, the poor man has to disappear into a quiet room with a plastic cup to watch pornography that is not of his own choosing! It's grossly unfair.

My chin begins to wobble even at the thought of it.

Lucky for us women, we have an amazing, informed medical profession ready to deal with our every issue, especially menopause. Right?

Maybe not right. Maybe closer to wrong.

I might have balls but, occasional beard aside, I am in no way a smaller man.

I'm a strong menopausal woman.

And like millions of others, I've been ignored by medicine.

CHAPTER 6

MEDICINE SANS GIVING A SHIT

I had been seeing various male GPs over the years, which I loved. But in my fifties, I decided that it was time I got myself a female doctor. Made sense. Women know women's bodies. She knew me, and she knew my body. Fantastic! Most importantly, she was a she, so I knew that she would be across the whole menopause thing. So, as soon as it dawned on me that that may be what was happening to me, I booked to see her at the first available appointment.

Throughout our lives, we have been heavily reliant on the status and knowledge of the medical profession to help us when we are in need of their expertise. And why not? It's not like women have been medically compromised. Just look at the statistics…Oh, wait, I shouldn't have clicked that link to the *Australian Institute Of Health and Welfare* from 2022.

56% of women have chronic health conditions

45% have experienced mental health issues

62,400 new cases of STIs reported in 2022

44,000 endometriosis related hospitalisations

58% of women lose more healthy years of life living with disease than from dying prematurely

Surely, the medical profession must be all over this, right?

Just let me click this other link and... oh...

Only 7% of medical research is focused on women's health.

Well, that's... no, it's not. It's not fair.

When statistics show that women live longer but suffer with more chronic pain and illness than men, you know we are being heavily disadvantaged. Resilience might be the new black, but discrimination is not, and never should be.

Australia's own health minister says he was 'astounded' that medical students spend as little as one hour of their entire courses learning about menopause. He might be astounded, but menopausal women aren't. Because of that, it's fair to say that there has been a dereliction of duty in way too many cases. Way too many women with symptoms like the ones I had have heard the same advice from the medical profession: "Exercise more, eat less and think about anti-depressants." In other words: "Get out of my office, you lazy, overindulgent mad bitch."

Not that that would happen to me.

When I finally had my appointment and outlined my symptoms and, more importantly, my suspicion that it was menopause, my doctor looked at me like I was crazy. She told me she doubted that was the case, her main reason being I was too old for menopause. Her advice, you guessed it: "Exercise more, eat less and think about anti-depressants."

I wasn't offered a hormone test.

I wasn't given options.

I was dismissed.

By a female doctor!

It's funny (but not) that erectile dysfunction is a bigger (pardon the pun — but not really) and more well known medical and social issue than menopause.

I remember years ago, it seemed that every second bus shelter, and billboards everywhere, had erectile dysfunction advertising plastered all over them.

The 1-800 Nasal Delivery technology ad: "Want longer lasting sex?" Or "Man Up": the Viagra campaign that had a 30-something handsome male in a business suit holding a gigantic hammer behind his head.

And then there was the 'Lovehoney' ad that had an image of a female hand holding a very long cucumber with the words: "Thanks to censorship we're getting creative. But let's face it, you deserve better."

I'm sorry, but phallic, over-exaggerated, extra-large cucumbers and huge hammers might be a priority for flaccid men, but they are in no way a priority for menopausal women. We are more concerned about the sandpaper between our legs, the fog in our brains, and the outrage flooding our veins. Now that would be an interesting image on a billboard.

When she was younger, Jamie was completely captivated by a particular burger ad. Unaccustomed as she was to the machinations of media savvy marketing magicians, just the sight of this flame-grilled wonder looked to her like Disneyland on a plate. Every time the ad would come on, she would instantly start salivating over this crafty creative work of edible art, and her own version of a sales pitch would start: "Mumma that looks so nice, doesn't it?" My reply would always be: "Yes, it does, but (insert gentle but sensible 'dinner' related reason here. For example, it's too close to dinner. We've already had dinner. Dinner's nearly ready, etc.)"

Finally, I got sick of feeling like I was sitting next to Pavlov's Dog every time this particular burger ad was aired and decided it was time she knew the brutal truth. "You know, Monkey, they don't really look like that."

Jamie looked at me, confused: "They don't?"

"Not really. They have a team of people who are paid to inject and finesse the burger and every other ingredient to make it look like it's the tastiest and best-looking thing you've ever seen. Oh, and they put food-safe 'shoe polish' on the bun to make it look glossy and perfectly brown."

"Shoe-polish? Yuk"

"Yep. Those burgers don't really look anything like that. They're mostly flat and limp and a little sad. They trick us so that we'll buy what they're selling us."

She paused for a moment, cocked her head to the side, and said: "Not buying. We're not buying!"

That became our motto. Now, anytime we see something that looks unrealistically appealing and that we know is trying to manipulate us or convince us of something we know is not true, Jamie launches into: "Not buying. We're not buying!"

As I drove home from my doctor's appointment, having succeeded in getting a blood test referral only by insisting on it, that phrase came to mind. "I'm not buying!"

So, guess what I'm not buying? This whole muted, misdiagnosing, menopause fiasco. And we women are buyers. We love to buy. We're buying plenty. We're buying more than men. So much more. And yet somehow women are grossly overlooked and unfairly underrepresented when it comes to most things medical. Why do we buy that? Why does the world buy that?

In 2024, *Time* magazine published an article about how women are still under-represented in medical research. They went on to state that, "as a result of this gender bias, insights into various diseases and findings about medications have often been extrapolated from men and applied to women. But women aren't just smaller men. Women's bodies are decidedly different from men's, with unique organs, genes, hormones, and other key differences."

When I read that, my first thought was: "I might have balls but (occasional beard aside) I am in no way a smaller man. I am a strong menopausal woman. And like millions of others, I've been ignored by medicine."

And, like the famous quote from 1996 movie *Network* goes: "I'm as mad (and as hot) as hell, and I'm not going to take this anymore!"

We pay others who should know more — medical 'experts' that we are told we can safely put our trust into. But when these doctors have only one hour of menopause training, then we are the ones that end up paying the price for that. The personal and physical fallout is huge. When I looked back on my own journey, however, I discovered that what I had experienced didn't start at menopause or perimenopause or even pre-menopause.

It might have started when I decided to have a child later in life than most and went through an IVF hellscape.

Or it might have started in early adulthood when I prioritised career over family.

Or it might have started in my late teens when I tried to unravel the tangle of sex and love and social expectations.

Or maybe it started in my early teens when hormones started treating my body like a disco and danced right through me.

Or, perhaps, it started in childhood when I'd get swept up in the joy of the moment and ignore bodily functions.

These are all the times I found myself in conflict with my body in some way or another. Sometimes this was due to ignorance or misinformation. Sometimes it was due to the fact that I, like most women, choose, or are forced, to prioritise others over our own bodies.

On rare occasions, this was because I was actually in pursuit of something that I wanted — independence, a career, financial security, love, a child.

By sheer luck or accident, I came to the conclusion that what I was feeling, this mysterious change in season, had to be menopause. But still, it took a lot of back and forth with various medical professionals to get an 'official' diagnosis.

However, even as this caused a sense of relief to wash over me — relief that I was not going mad, that I was not dying, that I would not have to kill my husband or assassinate any world leaders — I was still faced with the issue of why I was so unprepared for what is, after all, a natural thing that — and I'll say it again, in case you missed it the first time — happens to EVERY woman.

Maybe my mother was right? Maybe we don't count.

As Effie likes to say, "Greek women wear the pants, and wash and iron them too."

CHAPTER 7

IT'S NOT A BOY

People say life's not a competition. Unfortunately, the people that say that aren't old Greek women.

Old Greek women love to compete — over which one has the best house, the best husband, the best couch preserved in plastic. But the fiercest competition amongst Greek women, and not just the old ones, revolves around their kids.

There's the story of two older Greek women who meet up after not having seen each other since they were young girls in their village in Greece. For the sake of comedy and with no access to laser hair removal, let's call them Monobrow and Mutton Chops (not that I'm saying Greek women have an issue with facial hair, it's actually more of a whole-body problem).

Once they're done with reminiscing about old times and older friends, the competition starts, and Monobrow gets the upper hand with her three-storey, quadruple garage McMansion in the suburbs, a subservient husband with a full head of hair, and a couch that has never felt the ruinous touch of a human butt cheek without the protection of plastic sheeting.

Then, just when it looks like she's on the ropes and going down for the count, Mutton Chops asks: "So, do you have any children?". After a pause, in which Monobrow can't look Mutton Chops in the eye, she answers, "No… just three daughters." And Mutton Chops wins because she has a son. And even though he's forty-three, unemployed, still living at home and still "finding himself" — which he does a few times a day, though luckily his couch is also covered in plastic — Mutton Chops lands the knockout punch.

To truly understand that idea, you either had to be born in a remote Greek mountain village — or you could just be unlucky and be born a woman.

My mother was already a winner when she fell pregnant with me. Three years earlier, she'd had my brother, and he was bright and healthy and had an amazing head of hair. She was one for one. One pregnancy, one son. A perfect record.

Prenatal care being what it was in those days — non-existent — she had no way of knowing that her perfect record was about to be ruined until she actually held me in her arms. At which point, she showed all the enthusiasm of someone who has just opened a Christmas present from her partner, only to discover that it's a *Weight Watchers* cookbook.

So, while my ecstatic father was racing up and down the street handing out cigars to everyone he bumped into, my exhausted, disappointed mother lay in bed holding me and looking at me like I was a block of tofu. "If only back then I had the brain I have now," is my mother's response every time I bring up that story (which I do, frequently).

And when I think of her history and the mind-set she must have had, I totally get why, in her generational Greek eyes, having a girl was such a disappointment.

Exploring the ideas about menopause in different cultures is a wild ride. Reading about African, Indian, Islamic and Australian Indigenous cultures, as well as some ancient cultures, you tend to come across words and phrases like natural transition, wise womanhood, social freedom, women of wisdom.

It's only when you delve into Western (and some Asian) cultures that you start to meet words like taboo and decline, loss of femininity and even punishment being associated with menopause.

Among the worst, of course, are the Ancient Greeks.

The Greeks believed that men were powerful and perfect and that we women were weak and spongy. That's why women had periods, because their spongy absorbent bodies had to get rid of all the toxins they'd absorb. They also believed that when a woman went through menopause and lost her ability to squeeze out all the toxins she had soaked up that month, then those toxins would build up and she would become toxic and someone to avoid. I'd love to have a period now so I could expunge me some male toxicity on a regular basis.

And yet, regardless of so much of that backward and convenient thinking, Greek women still are remarkably strong. And they rule the roost. They know who's boss and what matters. They don't wait for the approval of males, historically or otherwise.

As Effie likes to say, "Greek women wear the pants, and wash and iron them, too."

I didn't ask my mother about her menopause till recently, after I realised what was happening to me. My mum claims that she hardly noticed it. That it was no big deal. Given that at the time she had just lost the love of her life and went into an extended period of mourning, this kind of made sense.

When you're in that much pain, you don't really have the energy to question the source of it. To her, the symptoms like the mood swings, the depression, the lack of sleep were about the loss of a loved one, not the loss of a bunch of hormones. And, I suppose, the developing desert down there made sense in the context that no one was interested in exploring that region anymore.

But given the culture in which she grew up and the journey she had, which was so male focused, I doubt she would have even discussed menopause, let alone sought help or treatment.

Now, before you start to form an image of a sheltered old Greek lady in your mind, let me assure you that my mother was anything but. Even in her mid-eighties she is one of the most switched-on people I have ever known. She may have all the hallmarks, *Deal Or No Deal* may be her favourite show, but her finger is definitely on society's pulse, and her gaydar is incredible. You should meet her.

Actually, here she is.

This working-class
version of
Sex And The City —
or in their case,
Sex And The Assembly
Line — was the source
of my mother's
knowledge of sex
and men.

CHAPTER 8

FANI. NOT FUNNY.

My mother's name is Fani.

One of her favourite things to say when meeting my friends for the first time is to anticipate their mispronunciation of her name: "I'm not funny, I am *Fani*. Mary — she's funny."

And given that she thinks it's a joke, she proves her own point that she is both funny and Fani. And it's true she is many things. Many contradictory things. Yes, she is traditional in some ways, but she's also playful, unpredictable, open, spontaneous, curious and very cheeky. Did I mention delusional?

Fani is a shortened version of Theofani which, in Greek, means the 'appearance of God' and Fani is certainly godly. Though she's barely 150 centimetres, she considers herself tall (which, according to her, she is compared to the other women from her village) and extremely good-looking (once again, we're comparing to a very limited field). While these both might be questionable claims, the 'godly' thing is, as she would put it, "One hundred percent!"

My mother exudes love. She has so much of it that she can't help but spread it into the world. Though she wouldn't stick out in a crowd because of her height or her supposedly stunning beauty, she immediately makes an impact everywhere she goes because she is an engine of pure joy. You instantly see Fani because she instantly sees you.

Fani was born in a very remote village in northern Greece which I am not allowed to name because she refers to it as "Ugly! Ugly!" (Fani likes to repeat things for emphasis.)

According to her, she was not only the brightest of her siblings, but everybody's favourite. She did well in school and even flirted with a career on stage after playing a communist in the school play, where her performance was so convincing, the local policeman came to her home to arrest her father. Fani was sure she had a life of glorious achievement stretching before her as maybe, a teacher? Maybe an actress? The possibilities were endless.

Then Fani turned fourteen and her older brother, the one who called the shots in the family, decided, "What you know already, is enough for a girl," pulled her out of school, and sent her to work in the fields picking cotton all day long. Back then, any task that a donkey couldn't do was a valid career path for a woman.

Fani's job was to earn enough money so that she didn't cost the family anything. Before there was ever such a thing as carbon neutral, there was woman neutral — where you made every effort to ensure your daughters weren't a drain on the family until you could marry them off.

And then that daughter could do that again for her husband and his often 'pain in the arse' family and before too long, the family they would create together.

Fani worked in those fields for three years, the highlight of which was a bus ride to Florina, the main town in the area, during which she locked eyes with a soldier who she thought was the most handsome man she had ever seen. She didn't talk to him. Good girls didn't do things like that, but he stuck in her mind because, "He had a face like cotton wool."

Whaaat?

Okay, follow her logic: a ball of cotton (with which she's had plenty of experience) looks like a cloud. Clouds float in the sky. The sky is where heaven is supposed to be. In other words, this guy's face was heavenly. And Fani never forgot him.

At the age of seventeen, she couldn't take it anymore, she felt she was spiritually suffocating working in those fields day after day and made the bold decision that she was destined for more — more what, she didn't exactly know.

Fani secretly wrote a heartfelt letter to a cousin in Australia, saying she wanted to leave the village and join her on the other side of the world. She was desperate to see what was possible there for her.

Months later, she made the bravest decision of her life. Fani lied about her age to get a passport and at '18' boarded a flight completely alone, flew for three days, stopping in five countries, eventually landing thousands of kilometres away in a place she knew nothing about with no education, no skills, no English. And no idea what challenges she was about to face. And all of that for the remote possibility of some freedom and the chance of something greater.

Instead, for the first two years she found herself in a factory six days a week, 12 hours a day, on a production line doing arduous, repetitive work to pay off her airline ticket debt. Not exactly freedom, but at least it was indoor work.

It was on that factory assembly line that she got the education she felt she had been denied from her multi-racial, multi-lingual, multi-talented factory worker mates.

Fani learned about the fickle nature of love from the Aussie woman whose husband dropped her off every morning with a kiss and an "I love you, I love you." It seemed like the ideal relationship to my naïve mother, until the day the woman showed up on her own, having discovered a note from her husband that said, "I don't love you anymore. I love somebody else." And she was left heartbroken, humiliated, and taking the train from that day on.

She also learned about the various complexities of sex.

From the Southern Mediterranean women, she learned about the power of withholding, as they taught her about rationing it out so the man wouldn't expect too much and be suitably grateful when he got it.

From the Eastern European women, she learned about what she innocently refers to as "trickya" — tricks you did in the bedroom to keep your man interested (none of which she ever considered doing, but that's a story my father could have told).

This United Nations working-class version of *Sex And The City* — or in their case, *Sex And The Assembly Line* — was the source of my mother's knowledge of sex and men. Along with recipes from a bunch of her Greek co-workers, an efficient mopping and washing-up technique, and strategic doily placement, it was the sum total of what she needed to know back then — as a woman.

As if sensing my mother's education was complete, her brother reached out across the vastness of the ocean and announced that it was time for her to get married. After all, she was almost twenty and getting a bit dusty on that shelf.

Fani knew and accepted that she would have no say in who she was going to marry. She trusted that between them, her brother and cousin would have the wisdom and good taste to choose a prospective groom for her.

They, of course had a stringent set of criteria that the groom had to fulfil in order to be 'good enough' for her. He had to be Greek, preferably breathing, and with all his parts. Ideally, he had to come from within ten kilometres of their 'ugly, ugly' village in Greece and, well, that's about it.

Dread has been a constant companion of mine throughout my life for lots of reasons that will no doubt be unearthed in this book, but the day my mother was due to meet her future husband, morbidly obese dread was sitting on her shoulder with a malicious grin on his face.

By the time the knock came on the front door and she went to answer it, Dread had brought along his cohort mates, Fear and Resignation. When Fani opened the door to meet her future husband, she couldn't believe her eyes: standing there was — the soldier from the bus in Greece, yes, the man with the cotton wool face. In that moment, my mother became an instant fan of arranged marriages, and she also became Mrs Cotton Wool.

Fani couldn't believe her luck. Here was the most beautiful man she had ever (nearly) met, and he turned out to be the most loving, supportive, hardworking and respectful partner, who believed, like her, that she was destined for more.

Throughout their marriage, my father never stopped pushing my mother to do more: learn to drive, strive for independence, explore the world around her. Soon, they had their own house, they had a successful business, and they had the perfect (note the penis) child. Her life was perfect.

Well, almost…

A couple of years after my brother was born, my father, at the age of thirty-three, had his first heart attack and though he recovered, it was the beginning of a battle he would be fighting his whole life and a race against time to prepare the three of us for a world without him. (Now you know where the Dread comes from.)

But that was all in the past, or in the future. As my mother held me in her arms that day, she only had one thought as she gazed into my puffy pink face, "What a shame it's not a boy."

Maybe this had something to do with the programming she got, that being a woman was somehow, not quite good enough. Or maybe she had just gone through so much herself that she couldn't bear the thought of her own child going through something similar.

Why bring a daughter into the world when what was in front of her was one brick wall after another to smash through?

Either way, before I was even conscious (which I define as being able to come up with a punch line), in the eyes of the people around me, my body was already defining me.

Before even formulating a thought, except for maybe, "Give me some of that milky tit" the packaging was more important than the product it contained. And, frankly, the packaging wasn't some plump, flame-grilled wonder, it was pinkish and puffy and, even that early, a little too hirsute.

If I had been capable of expressing myself, I think I would have told my mother not to worry because, as well as her genetic material, she had passed on a much more significant gift to me — a deep desire to find where I belonged and the depth of character and power to get there.

At least, I hoped so.

When getting back
on the horse, remember:

Sex isn't a charity.

If you're not getting off,
get off.

CHAPTER 9

SEX, SHLUCK SHLOOK AND THE EVIL EYE

If there's a currency amongst older Greek women that never loses its value, it's cleanliness. All roads, whether physical or domestic, are judged by one main thing: spotlessness. It represents honour, pride, talent, and worthiness.

I tell you this because what you will discover about my mother is that the words 'dirty' and 'clean' are frequently used, actually over-used slash abused, by her in many ways. The 'dirty bizzness' is how my mother refers to sex. She likes to call the downstairs department 'the dirty little birdie' or the 'stinky po-po.'

And like her kitchen bench, she's big on keeping that 'dirty bizzness' downstairs department clean: "I shluck shlook it twice a day, oh yeah. Its job is to get dirty. And it's our job to keep it clean."

As far as I'm concerned, sex, a bit like good looks, is something. It's not everything. But it's something that, at the right time with the right person, could be alright. Sometimes — hopefully a lot of the time — it could be great. But it could also be very underwhelming (more on that later).

Sex, however, should never be bad. Or wrong. Or used as a way to gain power. Or as a means to look for love. I know this for a fact because last time I checked, hearts and genitals were in different compartments.

As a child, I never got the sex talk. Did I want the sex talk? No, not really. Did I need the sex talk? Yes, absolutely. But did I need it from my mother? Probably not.

Did she have the talk with her mother about sex, safety, marriage, and motherhood before she left Greece at 17? No, she did not. Very few of them back then did. But what she did learn was that she was loved. And because of that, she knew how to love. That was enough of a great start.

My mother now isn't who she was fifty years ago. She's had her eyes opened by a big and often challenging life and had the privilege of intersecting with many great people along the way. People and conversations that have changed and liberated her. And because of that, she is driven to impact as much as she can on those she loves.

Her advice to Jamie, from one woman to another little woman, has always been: "Dimitra, don't you ever let someone touch your 'po po' until you are a big girl. Never. Never ever!"

My own personal advice to Jamie, when she's old enough to understand, will be, "Sex is not charity. If you're not getting off, then get off."

My mum's sage advice to me about sex and marriage was pretty basic: "Sometimes you don't feel like it. But after a while it's not so bad." I can't really argue with that.

My strong maternal grandmother's philosophy was even simpler than her sage daughter's: "A man should only know a woman from the waist down."

In other words, men have no business in knowing how we think. That was the marriage philosophy of a woman born in 1912.

When I heard that, it only further cemented my theory that Greek grandmothers were the original feminists — no bras, no hair removals, and no lack of balls.

All of those hilarious and pragmatic generational bits of advice are there to remind us of the power that we hold. They are the brilliant, gendered superglue that strengthens us. They are typically and traditionally awkward conversations that are now playful and quotable.

They are gold.

So much of what my mother equates as successful and virtuous involves a sponge, soap, and running water.

Those three things are her drugs of choice. She can't go a day without a hit. Sometimes twice a day. Especially when it applies to freshening up downstairs.

Euphemisms are her thing. She can't get enough of them, and neither can the rest of us. My mum's creative use of language is infectious. As onomatopoeia go, 'shluck shlook' is about as accurate and graphic as you can get. I won't go into too much detail describing the actual procedure other than to say it's a cross between a bird bath and a hand bidet situation. If you couldn't be bothered having a second shower, it can be carried out with one leg on the wall and the other on the floor, cradling a bathtub, and close to a tap and some soapy warm water. I think you get the picture. You'll be relieved to know there will be no Coustas: How to Shluck Shlook YouTube video available. You're welcome.

One of my favourite ways of teasing my mum to be her best feisty and funny self is by speaking to her in opposites.

The logic being that Greeks, like many ancient cultures, believe in the curse of the evil eye. The evil eye is essentially like bad vibes or too many good vibes but on steroids. The rationale is that any strong energy — it can be positive or negative feelings like jealousy or hate or awe or envy — that is thrust upon another could cause that other person to lose their physical or emotional equilibrium.

For example, when babies have bouts of unexplained distress, crying or vomiting, the Greeks attribute this to "mati" or evil eye. So, to protect the child from bad energy, Greek parents traditionally pin a tiny ornamental blue evil eye onto the child's clothing to act as a shield.

In popular movies like *My Big Fat Greek Wedding*, you'll see Greeks spit to one side of the person they are gushing over as a way of consciously not projecting the evil eye on them. This is a normal practice in Greek culture.

Because I love my playful, hilarious and addictive mum so much, I try to shield her from my positive evil eye vibes by speaking to her in opposites, in order to misdirect them from affecting her.

When I accuse my extremely morally sound mother of being a loose scarlet woman, my preferred line of teasing is:

"You are a filthy woman of the streets. Oh yeah, you are a dirty girl."

"I'm not dirty. I clean down there twice a day!"

"My point exactly! Why would you have to do it twice a day if it wasn't dirty?"

"Everyone's is dirty. Not just mine. Mine is cleaner than everybody else's because I 'shluck shlook' at least two times a day, oh yeah!"

Not typical mother/daughter conversation, I know, but it works for us because, in our family, we love jokes above all things.

As you might have already concluded, cleanliness (not just of the vaginal variety) in the Greek culture, is next to godliness. This is best illustrated by my mother's addiction slash obsession with the kitchen sink.

My father once said that if his wife was sent to a deserted island and she could take only three things, they would be: her pillow (she's the Michael Phelps of sleeping), her eyebrow pencil (they are anaemic and barely visible), and her kitchen sink. (As you've gathered by now, my mother has never met a sponge she didn't like.)

Growing up, we saw more of the back of my mother's head than we did her face.

When my brother and I built her new house, we made sure the kitchen sink was facing into the room, not out the window. We'd have lost her forever. Like any clean freak, my mother's excuse for living at that sink happily scrubbing away was, "The sink is like the whore of the village, it's always collecting dirty things!"

Yes, she was madly trying to emancipate that crockery, one filthy dish and pot at a time.

Sometimes I'd hear my mother on the phone with friends enthusiastically talking about cleaning, "This morning I put on the vacuum, I dusted the whole house, and I did two loads of washing. And when Stergio comes home, I'm going to clean the car, oh yeah." It was like her weekly SuperCoach catch up, hoping to outdo each other for bonus points.

My mum had strong opinions about other people's washing habits too. This was never better demonstrated than on the day my friend Sophie from school came over.

She was Greek, so she was very familiar with Greek mothers and their clean obsession. Her mother was next level. A daily deep-cleaning Hellenic Marie Kondo.

I was blown away by how immaculate Sophie's house always was. Their refrigerator was insane. You have never seen a more pristine, organised and decorated fridge in your life. Each shelf was covered in white plastic doilies laid out like little woggy wipeable coasters upon which the matching Tupperware happily sat. Truly breathtaking!

Sophie idly told me she'd just had a shower before coming over. My mum couldn't help jumping in, "It doesn't matter how much you wash your bum. A bum's a bum. It will always stink. That's its job!"

Even though Sophie's mother was an elite cleaner, she didn't see that one coming. No, that was a Fani Coustas special. Four decades later, Sophie says that whenever she showers, she recalls my mother's priceless words on the bum's natural propensity to stink.

And as history will testify, bums and Greeks go way back.

Yes, these pioneering Greeks discovered more than just Mathematics, Philosophy and Politics, they innovated in other ways too. The bedroom, for example. They apparently had few moral judgments around some of the illicit matters. As great orators and debaters, they also applied logic, and the principles of democracy to defend freedom of choice in the Anatomy department.

Thus, Homosexuality sits proudly beside Astronomy and Medicine as a field of human knowledge the Greeks took an early lead on.

Here's a modern day testimony of just how straightforward Greeks can be when it involves the back door.

A close friend sadly miscarried while holidaying on the Greek islands. She took an emergency flight to Athens. Lying in the hospital bed, feeling very low, with her partner standing beside her holding her hand, when Doctor Zeus walked in.

He was the best-looking man she had ever seen. George Clooney was a donkey next to this Greek God.

Suddenly, her spirits rose, as did her heartbeat. She felt an immediate overwhelming crush, alongside some mild shame.

The following dialogue was in Greek, which made it sound more poetic. In English, it sounds a little more graphic and unvarnished,

"I'm sorry for your loss. Very unfortunate. You'll be pleased to know that everything is fine. You might experience some cramping and light bleeding. That is normal. Do not do anything strenuous for the next few days. Any questions?"

My friend no doubt wanted to ask, "Yes, can I have your phone number?" But she didn't.

Instead, she asked, somewhat flustered, "Sex… Is it okay to have sex?"

Doctor Zeus didn't skip a beat:

"Yes, no problem. Just not in the front hole."

He was serious.

Pragmatic advice that further affirms the only time Greeks refuse to be squeaky clean is in the bedroom.

But at the heart of this sentiment, along with my mother's 'shluck shlook' philosophy, is the notion that the vagina when not kept in check, could lead you to some very unhygienic and hairy situations.

From an early age I was convinced that I was walking around with a ticking time bomb down there and one day, if I wasn't careful, it would explode.

So, when I turned eighteen, two important things happened, 1) I got my driver's licence, and 2) it was time to decommission the ticking bomb in my pants.

Not because I was overwhelmingly physically attracted to someone. Nor was I bursting with sexual energy or curiosity. No, I simply felt I had to do it.

The 1972 Labour Party campaign slogan echoed my feelings exactly. *"It's Time."* Gough Whitlam famously told the nation. And me. I simply decided it was time.

At 18, I finally found my artistic forever tribe. I was accepted into acting school at Deakin university and began living away from home in a share house full of amazing people — actors, musical performers, free spirits. Young talented people who were both inspiring and horny.

Rooting, the technical term we used back then, was rampant. It was happening all around me, in every corner of our house, and it was loud and energetic. Naturally, I felt I needed to put rooting onto the agenda.

Sex hadn't been a high priority, given my limited experience. In high school, I had a friend who was let's say, very progressive, very forward…she was definitely leading the pack. She was my version of the Eastern European factory women and their fancy 'trickya'. She was coincidentally, Estonian. Let's call her Estonia, for confidentiality reasons.

When I asked Estonia what she did exactly with the boys I didn't get the lurid details I was hoping for. She was so matter-of-fact in her attitude, "it was no biggie". She made sex seem a little boring and functional to me.

I wonder how different my entrée to sex might have been if my blasé friend had used more explicit adjectives. Words clearly weren't her forte.

Randy Estonia did offer me, however, a complete physical re-enactment, step-by-step, thrust-by-thrust, during a sleepover at her place.

Estonia was keen to play the part of her Turkish boyfriend and invited me to play her. I respectfully declined. Not because I was prudish, I just didn't think I could play the role of a tall blonde horny Estonian convincingly. Plus, I wasn't feeling any tingling Mexican wave. 'No biggie'.

Months after the proposed re-enactment, things took an unexpected and dramatic turn. Walking home from school one day, she confided that she was pregnant. She was going to have it "taken care of" the following day. She asked if I would go to the clinic with her on the bus, and I said okay.

I hardly slept that night. Not because I was wrestling with any moral dilemma. I was worried about how she would afford the doctor? Did her parents know? Would they pay? From watching B-grade American films I knew that such things were notoriously dodgy, expensive affairs. In those movies, the poor girl would have to 'work the streets' to get the money needed. And that's when things would get really bad.

As usual, this episode turned out to be 'no biggie' for my matter-of-fact friend. We caught the bus into the city. I waited as she walked in with a blank expression on her face. She came out with the same expression on her face. We never talked about it. We caught the bus home. And because she lived closer to the bus stop than I did, she gave me a dink home on her Dragstar bike.

Clueless children dealing with adult issues and talking to no one.

The pattern of silence starts somewhere.

Three years later, I made a matter-of-fact, unmindful decision to end my virginity. I decided, enough, "It's Time."

I called one of my best male friends and asked if he was busy and would he like to come over? Our relationship thus far had been strictly 'friends zone', I was sharing a house in Geelong and he was an hour away in Melbourne. So he started with the excuses. Then I strongly hinted at what was on my agenda.

Forty minutes later, he was at my front door.

Things didn't really go as planned. Not that I had any detailed plan besides getting the job ticked off my To-Do list. With zero romance and no emotional element, two complete novices, with no genuine physical attraction, got the job done. It all fell a bit flat.

My first anti-climax.

If I had to squeeze out an adjective, it would be 'functional', but I don't think that's appropriate because it contains the word 'fun' in it, and there was nothing fun about it. It was sex, but far from sexy. The lack of heat and the abundance of awkwardness were totally working against us.

After that, I decided that when it came to sex, I was going to listen to my body and my heart and not my housemates and their regular loud humping.

I spent the next eighteen months diligently and somewhat unnecessarily, 'shluck shlooking' and waiting for my body to give me a sign.

I would love to say that when I finally got back on the horse it was a magical, mind-blowing, life-changing experience, but I'm struggling to remember it, so it couldn't have been. But it definitely got better and better. And here's what I thankfully found out: when things are in synch — mind, body, heart — sex is really something.

It's not everything, but it is something.

Which is helpful to keep in mind during menopause.

I keep being reminded of my mum's basic, pragmatic view of what sex can be: "Sometimes you don't feel like it. But after a while it's not so bad." Not so bad? It should never be even remotely bad. Or painful. Ever.

Sex during menopause can be uncomfortable. As I like to say, "I used to be dessert. And now I'm a desert."

Hallelujah for lubricants.

For others, menopause can mean a decreased libido, which raises the question: "How low can you go?"

The answer to that is different for every person. All these things leave you weighing up whether it's all worth it or not. And that's worth contemplating.

But if you can see past the rigmarole and if your body and mind and whatever treatment you are using is helping get you back on track, then there's every chance you'll get there. You will.

And if, in good faith, you have committed yourself wholeheartedly to getting back on that lubricated horse — or Shetland pony if that's more applicable — and it's still not working for you, just remember my advice to Jamie:

Sex isn't a charity. If you're not getting off, then get off.

You realise
that your downstairs
pink slip has turned into
the Sahara Desert
instead of its former
Wet'n'Wild self.

CHAPTER 10

THE 34 SYMPTOMS OF MENOPAUSE — AND WHY THEY'RE MOSTLY GEORGE'S FAULT

My original opening sentence for this section was going to be. "When I finally realised I was going through menopause…" And as soon as it was on the screen, I immediately deleted it.

The phrase 'going through' doesn't feel right for a few reasons. Yes, it describes the painful and debilitating reality of menopause, but it also buys into all that cultural myth of it being a sort of hormonal death sentence.

Personally, I wouldn't call it death exactly. Yes, my hormones have diminished dramatically, no arguing that. I prefer to describe it as being hormonally dehydrated. Thankfully, MHT (Menopausal Hormone Therapy) has come to my rescue and I've been able to top them up or in more melodramatic terms, I've put my hormones on permanent life support.

Yes, it's the end of an era. But there are many eras we have to say goodbye to in life. And for me, the best news about menopause is there are no more periods, and I have to say I'm thrilled about that. That body-aching, red sea of inconvenience was a monthly challenge I do not miss at all.

Throughout the years, we watch our bodies change, morph and ready themselves for miraculous feats. And each of those stages comes with much pain, discomfort, confusion, and growth. This stage is no different, except for one thing: it doesn't get spoken about nearly enough. And because of that, we are caught off guard. We are way too regularly left in the dark about something we should have always been prepared for.

My issue with the term "going through menopause" is that it implies that it will, at some point, be over. But hey, who are we kidding? Those hormones aren't coming back. Our ovary factory has stopped producing eggs and because of that, it's significantly reduced its production of reproductive hormones. And the result of that is body and brain bedlam. Everything is scrambling.

Suddenly, those usually reliable hormonal couriers can't deliver what we need them to. Which leads to turmoil. And that is no easy thing to 'go through', especially when that 'going through' is permanent.

So, you do everything you can to manage it. And you find a way to control it instead of it controlling you. The best way to take control is to talk about it. And I did.

Don't get me wrong, it wasn't like, "Hey Mary, how's it going?"

"Well, I'm glad you asked. Have I got a depressing long menopausal story for you! Give me an hour of your time and I'll take you through the short version."

No, it was not that. But it wasn't something I hid any longer, and when it did come out organically, other women's stories followed suit. And most women had a story that was unnecessarily difficult and, like me, most of them had been lost in the fog of helplessness for way too long.

As soon as menopause became common knowledge in our household, there was a collective sigh of relief, and the one who sighed loudest wasn't me. It was my husband, George.

He was deeply relieved that I finally identified what was happening to me. George immediately connected me with a friend who had operated menopause clinics in the US.

He also encouraged me to start writing about these recent experiences, as I did a decade before, which gave birth to my first memoir, *All I Know*, primarily about grief and loss. I wanted to help lift the veil on my difficult menopause journey, as I strongly suspected I was not the only one struggling with it.

So, we read and listened to as much as we could about the subject. Like me, George was in complete disbelief that such a huge thing like menopause is still way too regularly misdiagnosed and swept under the shameful, stigmatised and uninformed rug.

But to be honest, I suspect the main reason George was so relieved, is that now, in his mind, he has a justifiable reason to believe he did nothing wrong for all those years. That none of it was his fault. That he was perfect and right, and my every reaction to everything can now be blamed on menopause.

Suddenly, for George, menopause has become a get-out-of-jail-free card. If I was him, I wouldn't be leaving the country any time soon because, just quietly, his fingerprints were still considered evidence.

My personal get-out-of-menopause-jail card was information. I was on a hunt to find the right doctor and other professionals to help get me back into balance and resume my life.

So many ambitions were still sitting in storage, wondering when I was going to unlock the cage. I had the key now and was desperate to finally fling the menopause door open and come out of the hormonal closet.

I trawled through the seemingly infinite symptoms so I could get my foggy head around them all. First came the 34 common ones: "Whoa, baby, please stop." And then I did a deep dive: "Oh my God, I'm drowning, please somebody help me" into the over one hundred combined common and lesser-known symptoms. And that's when I started to lose my will to read, breathe, but oddly not eat.

Discovering the impact of fleeing hormones on a woman's body was both eye-opening and overwhelming. The best part was I could tick off a few symptoms, and that was reassuring, but still there were plenty of others that were news to me, ones that I had never had or even heard of in relation to menopause. And yet there were some things I was feeling physically and emotionally that weren't on any list.

Was it menopause? Was it something else? Was it something else and menopause? If so, what was the something else? (For a full list of suspects, see THE INSIDE JOB section). And if that was the case, how much of my misery was being caused by this 'something else' and how much was menopause?

These questions were totally baffling. Why did it seem that my experience of menopause was in some ways textbook and in other ways completely unique?

And, then it hit me. That 'something else'… was sweet, innocent George.

And not just George, my darling daughter Jamie too. And all those other factors, internal and external, I listed earlier. And the whole bloody world at times. And everything in it that was divisive, destructive, and depressing — and there's been plenty of that in the last ten years.

But mostly, he wouldn't hurt a fly (a mosquito, on the other hand…) good guy George.

It's like when they interview a neighbour on *A Current Affair* and she says, "He was a nice man, kept to himself most of the time."

I don't want to imply that everything is George's fault. I mean — and this may sound obvious — that menopause doesn't happen in isolation. Familial, psychological, physical, cultural, social, and way too often genital factors only add to the discomfort and complexity.

You're desperate to get that unroadworthy old banger, off the blocks and back on the road, only to realise that your downstairs pink slip has turned into the Sahara Desert instead of its former Wet'n'Wild self.

George still sometimes plays the "it's the menopause" card. Which is ridiculous because, as far as I can tell, 'the menopause' isn't the reason he's not home on time to pick up our daughter from school when I'm busy.

Nor is 'the menopause' to blame for the mood he's in when Manchester United loses a football game.

And I'm almost a "hundred percent" sure that 'the menopause' isn't the reason that George isn't getting a good night's sleep.

And George does everything humanly possible to make sure he gets great sleep, every single night.

George is one of the most accomplished people in his profession. He has worked as a copywriter and creative director for massive ad agencies in Sydney and New York and established his own very successful agency. Not bad, considering that advertising is George's side hustle, because his main job is getting 'good' sleep.

George's pre-bed routine involves everything from machinery to mantras, where everything from his breathing to the temperature of the bed must be just right in order for him to get to sleep. It has to be the right room temperature, the right pillow, the right sheets, the right duvet weight. I think you get that everything has to be 'right'.

He disdains the ignorant among us who just put our heads on pillows and just expect it to happen. His precision is military, and his dedication is legendary. NASA's check list to get a rocket to the moon is nothing in comparison.

He loves to start the day with his favourite subject, sleep scrutinisation. Seconds after he opens his eyes he hits me with the question, "How did you go?" And my response to that, for all those years pre-menopause, was, "I think I did okay. I closed my eyes. I went to sleep. And now I just opened them."

Since menopause, he doesn't dare ask the question. But somehow, I still have to hear about how he slept. It appears to be of such grave 'importance' that I'm contemplating asking *Channel 9* to include it on the six o'clock news, alongside the Dow Jones figures. No doubt the public would be desperate to know the ups and downs of George's sleeping stock exchange.

And while I've learned to accept that my husband's real career is getting to sleep, I could do without the running commentary, which is more than a little irritating.

This begs the question: "What does that have to do with the mood swings you might experience during menopause?" And the answer is, "Not much." It can cause some of those moods to swing a little more. And as funny and cute as it is at times, it's irritating all by itself.

There is no arguing that mood and irritability can be due to menopause, but there are other stressful factors, big and small, that affect your life. And then there's… you guessed it, George.

So, keep those things in mind as you look through the list of symptoms and possible symptoms of menopause you might be experiencing below. (Please feel free to substitute your partner's name each time you see my husband's.)

Let's start with the symptoms everyone knows:

Irregular periods — They might get heavier or lighter than usual, you might skip a few, they might not come as regularly as they did, or become more painful. But they're George's fault.

Hot flashes — Eighty percent of us cop them. Sudden heat, sweating, and chills that can go for a minute or five or more. George does love to fiddle with the temperature control on our heating system…

Night sweats — These are the hot flushes you have at night, where the sweating soaks the sheets and suddenly, you're freezing. Either way, you sure aren't sleeping. Meanwhile, Mr Apnoea-Awareness is dreaming away and making it even worse.

Insomnia — If the night sweats aren't keeping you up enough, then we have its little aiding and abetting mate, insomnia, to rely on. Yes, plenty of us (between 40%-50%) know that 'mate' which is far from friendly. And then, adding pain to injury, Professor Sleep Dude a foot away generously chucks in some snoring free of charge as a little garnish of irritation.

Vaginal Dryness — Okay, this one's a little harder to pin on George, but I'm sure the one in five women over the age of 43 who experience it can help me find something. All I would say to this is, it's hard to keep the tap turned on when there's a drought.

Mood Swings — Known factors include hormonal shifts, exhaustion from all the insomnia and night sweats, and of course, listening to George. And somehow still being highly functional even though you're barely functional.

Weight gain — At the rate of about half a kilo a year for women aged between 45 and 55 years old, which is as much to do with loss of muscle mass as it does with hormones and George's insistence on gravy with everything. Damn that gravy and my menopausal middle-aged metabolism.

Then there's what I like to call the big three psychological ones:

Memory lapses, Depression, Anxiety — They can all cause feelings of dread, hopelessness, and nervous anticipation, and the change to estrogen and progesterone levels may lead to them. As do George's daily rants on the health benefits of goat's milk and the many shortcomings of his favourite NRL team, mostly due to overpaid and under-delivering players.

These are also factors in the experience of symptoms such as: Irritability and Fatigue.

However, as you delve further into the symptoms, George's impact begins to diminish as estrogen rears its rapidly departing head more and more.

Estrogen is a hormone, a little chemical messenger that is as vital to your sexual and reproductive health as a nosy old Greek woman is to spreading gossip through a village. And, jeez, can it talk.

Its link to cognitive function is a major contributor to about 60% of menopausal women experiencing Brain Fog — having sudden memory lapses or spacing out.

Low libido, is associated with decreased levels of both estrogens and androgens, resulting in decreased sexual arousal.

Estrogen's role in maintaining healthy skin can result in itchiness.

Food sensitivities/IBS (Irritable bowel syndrome) may also be linked to estrogen, due its role in helping to manage visceral sensitivity and intestinal function.

Bloating may occur because of fluctuating levels of estrogen and progesterone can cause fluid retention (which is obviously what happened to my mother's ankles).

Strange Food Cravings may become an issue because high estrogen levels in the brain are linked with feeling full after eating.

Then there are the various physical symptoms such as Headaches, Joint Pain, Muscle Aches and Tension, Breast Tenderness, all impacted by dropping estrogen and progesterone levels and adding to the poor sleep and stress.

Then there's the weird ones like — Paresthesia, where you experience a tingling sensation like pins and needles — Burning Mouth Syndrome, which can also lead to changes in how things taste; or the sensation of feeling Electric Shocks.

As far as I know, all of these are less common physical symptoms, but all could indicate underlying conditions and should really be discussed with your doctor — that is, if you can find a good one that knows about menopause.

The list continues: Thinning Hair, Brittle Nails, Dizzy Spells, Incontinence, sudden new Allergies, Osteoporosis, and even Irregular Heartbeat.

Given all these issues and symptoms, it's no wonder so many women experiencing menopause suffer from Panic Disorder or Panic Attacks. Symptoms of panic attacks include: chest pain, shortness of breath, heart palpitations, dizziness, and so on, and can spiral so that you feel you're losing your mind.

Of course, you are, with some or all of that to contend with.

Not to mention a George or two in your life and the list of other demanding humans, work commitments, and responsibilities.

How do things get easier for us women? How do we prioritise ourselves without all the demanding responsibilities slash house of cards falling down?

I'm grateful that there are great people doing great work in the menopause space. But there needs to be more.

Personally, I wanted to do more than just talk or write about menopause. Yes, I wanted to draw attention to a problem, but more than that, I wanted to offer a solution. But I knew I couldn't do that without the help of others.

And then boom! Cut to: four incredible women turning up.

All fellow menopausal sufferers, all with their own stories, all looking to do something professionally that spoke to their own difficult journey and that made a difference to others. Sound familiar?

One a managing director, another a registered nurse, another a 'get-great-shit-done' operations manager slash producer and last but never least, an incredible fertility doctor slash gynaecologist who knows hormones like I know jokes.

Our mission was: to make something hard a lot easier.

We wanted to create a practical, easy way for women to get the medical care they needed.

All that was left to do was get on our high-vis outfits and marshal menopausal women from anywhere Australia to our online tele-health practice and have our great doctors help them.

I think I speak for all women when I say, I'd rather shop for shoes, than doctors.

Finding my gun women was exactly what I needed.

Thank God for the sisterhood. They deliver just like all those previous hormones we took for granted.

Except there's one huge difference: unlike hormones: a great posse of women never leave you. Amen sisters!

The sad truth is, when you're a Greek chick – it's Movember every month.

CHAPTER 11

DISCOVERING THE SISTERHOOD

Every woman — and before that, girl — has had to deal with the cramps, the breast tenderness, the mood swings, the bloating, the headaches, the fatigue, the acne. Yes, I speak of the joyous gifts of menstruation. Not to mention the constant fear of leakage…

Probably the most difficult thing I faced was: what the hell was going on? I wasn't totally blind. I'd picked up scraps from hushed school yard chats. But it all sounded terrifying and raised more questions than answers.

Bleeding for days? Why? What did I do to deserve that? What could I do to avoid it? Where did all the blood go? How many days? What do I put between my legs? Or up the other hole that I didn't even know I had?

I got my first period in grade six, at age eleven. I've blocked out any memory of it and, given the minute detail with which I can recall some other moments of bodily functions gone wild, I figure it was either 'no biggie' or so horrific my brain pretended it just didn't happen. I prefer to go with the 'no biggie' scenario.

I do remember the day when I finally told my mother about it. She, however, said as little as possible, reached into a drawer, and then shoved something the size of a small surfboard in my face. Then she handed me two safety pins and told me to attach the humongous pad to my big, ugly period undies that just happened to look identical to hers.

"Please God, don't tell me I'm wearing my mum's massive panties? As if bleeding wasn't enough!!!"

"C'mon, put it on!", she said. "Put it on?" I could ride that thing! How was I supposed to walk with it between my legs?

Eventually, my schoolyard chick posse let me in on the latest innovation: sanitary pads with wings. Wings!!! I couldn't get to Coles fast enough. Finally, no more looking like I had half a dozen footy socks shoved down my pants (that was my brother Con's thing — not really, but I couldn't resist.)

Not long after that, I was introduced to the wonders of 'shluck shlook'.

What's ridiculous is that nobody thought to explain what was actually happening to my body at that age, the possible repercussions, or the physical and mental issues and embarrassments that might arise.

It wasn't until years later, in Health Ed, that we learned words like ovulation, endometrium, estrogen, progesterone, and follicles (so many bloody follicles). And it didn't help much because by then our mindset was, "Just shut up and pretend it isn't happening."

And I can't help thinking that the innovations in women's 'sanitary products' (you can tell a man came up with that term) which took them from pads the size of Lilos and tampons that put most North Korean missiles to shame, to the discreet, slimline, undetectable things with wings

— were less about the comfort and effectiveness for women and more about making sure there's nothing to see here.

Initially, I didn't understand that concept. I considered myself an educator, much more mature than most kids, and now I finally had confirmation of that maturity. I felt it was time that people knew that. Especially Rod and Todd.

But before we get into that, I think I need to establish my dedication to education.

Young teachers get terrorised at schools. Mainly because their students are even better at smelling fear than dogs. And before the days of PlayStations, the only buttons you had to push belonged to the adults around you — especially insecure twenty-somethings that were trying to teach you English or science or anything at all for that matter.

Even as a kid, I couldn't stand to watch the torment, so I did my best to make them feel better about themselves. My mother wanted to be a teacher when she was a young girl in the village. And I did too. So I had a soft spot for them.

When they crapped on about Captain Cook and half the class was dozing off, and the other half were daydreaming and looking out the classroom window, I nodded enthusiastically, trying to maintain what would be referred to in a sales seminar as 'good eye contact'.

When they asked their pointless questions, my hand was always the first to shoot up with the answer. And when the bell rang at the end of class, I would avoid the wildebeest-like stampede for the door and just linger, just a little bit, to smile at the teacher and let them see my silent appreciation of their great work.

Yes, there were whispers in the corridor as I passed, "Suck up… teacher's pet… crawler…" I ignored them. I knew it was true though. How can you argue with the truth? I even came to wear those labels like a badge of honour, knowing that I, almost single-handedly, was preventing mental breakdowns and floods of frustrated, insecure tears from taking place in the staff room.

I was like the Mother Teresa of junior teachers — except I didn't have to deal with all that poverty and starvation. Also, my outfit was far more fashion-forward than M. Teresa's.

Just quietly, no, I didn't have many friends. I had to accept whether I liked it or not that "less is more" — or, on tougher days that if 'less is more,' then does that make, 'none is less than less and therefore even more?' I didn't think so.

I was lucky that at home I had my loving parents, very loyal border collie, 'Fonzie' as well as my older brother, the afore-mentioned golden boy, Con. Who, too, was a dog sometimes.

Con and I spent most of our childhood either super close or super cheesed off at each other. When we were in harmony, Con was the best brother anyone could hope for — always including me in the games and adventures he would have with his friends, making sure I was always safe from harm.

Aside from those two days, however, Con and I were in a constant state of cold war. Or, as I like to call them, our cold meat and cheesy charcuterie board periods. At those times, we were ruthless with each other.

Speaking of charcuterie, one Saturday after my parents had been to the Victoria Market and bought the most delicious fresh produce and cold meats, Con immediately grabbed the whole Hungarian salami, complete with string. I asked if I could cut myself a slice. Con, seeing how much I wanted it, dangled it from its string and pulled it away from me, uttering the extremely annoying words, "Coo chi coo chi coo." I asked again and reached for it, only for Con to lift the salami even higher and repeat the most infuriating words ever heard, "Coo chi coo chi coo."

This went on and on. Finally, broken by this brotherly torture, I admitted defeat and retreated to the lounge room for rest and revenge regeneration. When Con had headed out to play, I hit that fridge and Hungarian Salami like it was nobody's business.

Later that night, in the bedroom I shared with my adoring brother, my stomach began to pay the price for my gluttonous actions. Gurgling and churning, with bile rising in my throat, I called out to my loving brother, "Con... Con I feel sick."

Con's loving response? "Stiff shit! Go tell Mum and Dad."

Disappointed but not shocked, I got out of bed and stumbled, doubled over with pain, towards the door — right next to which was Con's prized possession, his guitar.

Hello Dolly.

The perfect revenge opportunity revealed itself. Without any prompting, my body performed like the spewing star that it is, and I vomited into the hole of my brother's beloved guitar. Bullseye, baby.

In the words of Effie, "Good thanks!"

To say Con was 'spewing' himself is a gross understatement.

From that genius moment of mine onwards Con decided to practice his Bruce Lee karate moves on me at every opportunity. Me? I didn't care — as far as I was concerned — it was so worth it.

Con was also a fan of humiliating me with a 'surprise attack.' I'd done a bit of that myself so 'no biggie'. He knew that I was more competent verbally, so he had to get in quick and hit me with a knockout blow.

One evening, with the whole family seated at the dinner table, relaxing after a meal. Out of nowhere, Con pointed at me and announced: "You've got a moustache! What are you, a man?"

I wish I'd snapped back with, "And you've got a monobrow. What are you, Frida Kahlo?" But I didn't. Partly because I was stunned …and partly because at twelve, I had no idea who Frida Kahlo was.

So instead, I deployed the most potent weapon in my arsenal: stretching the word Dad over five syllables.

"Da-a-a-a-a-d!" Then I melodramatically bolted to the bathroom.

As my father told Con off, I stared into the mirror, forensically scrutinising my top lip. Surely, Con was wrong. Surely it was just a trick of the light…

The sad truth is, when you're a Greek chick — it's Movember every month. There it was, plain as day: the hungry, hairy caterpillar.

Stunned and speechless, I grabbed my father's Remington razor and shaved that thing right off. It's not a method I would now recommend.

I don't know whether it's just an urban myth that the hair grows back thicker, but let's just say in the intervening years bleach has become my friend. Not that bleach is foolproof either. Leave it on too long and you've suddenly got a peroxided Annie Lennox sitting on your upper lip.

That comment from my brother — and an even more socially scarring incident a week later — only further confirmed what I feared: my body had become a follicular franchise, with bushels of hairs sprouting from a variety of inconvenient locations.

As a devoted fashionista, what I wore to school was important to me. My favourite outfit was a paisley halter-neck dress that I wore whenever I could.

I've already spoken of my charitable work with young teachers, which meant my arm was always the first that shoot up when they asked a question. On this occasion, when I raised my arm to enthusiastically answer a question about Sir Joseph Banks (botanist, by the way), I inadvertently revealed huge tufts of underarm mohair to the entire class.

It was met with an Anglo chorus of appalled:

"Oh yucks"

"Hairy Mary!!!"

"Ergghhh that's disgusting"

High pitched giggles. Humiliating finger pointing. Worst of all, even the teacher was hiding a grin.

In the words of Effie, "How embarrassment."

I was faced with a dilemma — find a solution or let my increasingly bushy body ruin my education.

The Remington option was briefly on the table, but instead I opted for something else. No, not abandoning the halter neck — I had a duty to my imagined public to continue wearing it.

Instead, I developed a technique: raise one arm while cupping my opposite hand over the thicket of sprouting underarm hair.

Simple, elegant, fashionable, and in no way stupid looking.

Even then, I knew enough about puberty to know that this sudden follicular flourish was just the beginning. Not that I had consulted anyone about it or had been informed about it at all. I knew things were coming down the pipeline that might even be more of a challenge, but I had no idea what. It still wasn't part of the school curriculum — and wouldn't be until I was well into my teens, which I call the 'shutting the gate after the horse has bolted and taken all the tampons' school of education.

Also, any conversation with my mother about these matters was pointless. She herself was not a student of female grooming. Put it this way: the only thing my mother had ever shaved was parmesan cheese. Again, I was stranded, left to my own pathetic devices, internet-less and relying on the kindness of members of the hairy sisterhood — of which there were not many.

I lived in Anglosville. And no, that's not a suburb; it's a reality of some suburbs. Being one of the few Wogs at my school meant that I had to seek out help from friendly chemist staff to help me with my fleecy, fuzzy predicament.

Jenny from the local Amcal chemist suggested I try Nair — a product that was first created in the 1940s made up of chemicals with names like potassium thioglycolate and calcium hydroxide. I decided against it very early because it felt too much like napalming my face.

I loved my mum, but truth be told she was not great value when it came to the various 'surprises' my body had in store. I learned very quickly that I had to depend on my own ingenuity to get me through. I would have to improvise with whatever I could from that point on to spare me from further humiliation. The good news was that, for the moment, my main hirsute arm pit issue had been taken care of.

The natural and novel hand-cupping technique was a big win. Mary 1, Body 0.

Now, back to Rod and Todd and my enlightening slash educational agenda…

They were two of the cool guys in school. They played footy, teased teachers in class, and rocked surfie haircuts. Rod had a leather necklace with a genuine shark's tooth; Todd's face was dappled with beautiful cinnamon freckles. I had a crush on both and didn't know which one to choose. I could tell they were both interested in me too.

In the end, I decided I'd go with the one that was the more mature. And my genius test? Sit with them at lunchtime and tell them everything that was going on with my period. That way, they'd know they were dealing with a "woman" who understood the ways of the world — not just a girl. The more mature of the two would step up to take on the job.

Unfortunately, it didn't go that way.

Maybe I was too forensic in my detail. Because by the time I finished telling them about bleeding, leaking, supermarket shelves loaded with pads and tampons as far as the eye could see, and how their mothers, sisters and female teachers were all experiencing the same thing — and which girls in school it was also happening to — neither Rod, nor Todd ever made eye contact with me again.

Todd's beautiful cinnamon freckles had disappeared under a blush of bright red. Rod's shark tooth pendant hung limp down his chest.

And it got even more awkward. Rod lived across the road from my one of my best friends. Every time I went to visit her, Rod and his brothers and their mates would be playing footy or cricket or in the street. I could feel them looking at me. I knew I'd lost Rod — that wasn't the issue. The issue was that I'd also ruined my chances with Rod's older brother, who was a dead ringer for David Soul from "Starsky and Hutch."

Lesson learned: menstrual musings should be confined to the sisterhood.

By the time we hit high school, that's exactly what we did. We became each other's insurance policy — checking for blood stains, lending jumpers to tie around the waist and keeping spares in lockers for anyone who got 'flooded' or got caught by surprise.

Suddenly, despite all our differences, every girl at school was united by two ideas:

- That we were all going through the same thing — and
- Only sluts used tampons — and no one wanted to be the slut with the Super.

In retrospect, my conversation with Rod and Todd was also a valuable lesson for me as a performer. Know your audience and adjust your material accordingly.

Next time I'll use PowerPoint… complete with diagrams, bullet points and maybe even a Q&A session.

Since then, I've relied on the posse for sharing advice, information, and understanding. Over the years, we have compared and contrasted bumps, lumps, emissions and emotions and they have rarely let me down.

So, it was a shock to learn that some sisters — or cousins in this case — can let you down.

Was he having a stroke, or had some kind of noxious sea creature latched onto my T-shirt?

CHAPTER 12

WET T-SHIRT MARY

One of my character Effie's *"Effiemations"* — the things she says to herself in the mirror every morning to buoy her spirits — is: "We women need to be each other's bras. We need to support and uplift each other so we can be pert and upright."

Effie is a huge believer in the sisterhood, and so am I. When your body was going haywire, it was someone from the sisterhood — the girls at your school or in your family — who set you straight.

From that well of womanhood, you learned not to squeeze your pimples lest you scar your skin. Not that I could resist. Especially those big boilers. How could anyone leave one of those alone? And let's be honest, is there anything as deeply satisfying as that massive squirting pop? It was the sisterhood, the lady legends, your pussy posse that also gave you advice about greasy hair, oily skin, off odours — how to hide or treat the various bumps and sticky, stinky bits that had suddenly become your body.

Ironically, it was a friend's brother that recommended one of the most useful products ever created for self-conscious, pubescent girls and their 'intimate skins'. My friend Peta lived around the corner from us in suburban Doncaster with her mum, dad, and two brothers.

Her younger one was still in primary school — beneath our notice. But the oldest? Infamous. The rumour was that he was, as my mother would say, "on drungs" which made him a "drungaholic". Maybe he was, maybe he wasn't — (Okay, he was — 100%.) What I knew for sure was he was a funny, inappropriate, charismatic guy and constantly chain-smoking.

Whenever he ran out of cigarettes, he'd hand Peta some cash and send her to the milk bar to get him a packet. He always gave her extra money, so she'd score herself a Pollywaffle, a packet of Samboy chips, or a cold can of creamy soda.

One afternoon when I was at their house, Peta's mother asked, "Mary, do you wanna stay for tea?" — which I quickly found out meant dinner.

"Yeah, I'd love to Mrs G."

"Great, someone please set a place for Mary!"

While the plates and cutlery were hitting the table I watched Mrs G — a chain smoker herself — mash the potatoes with an ash-laden More cigarette dangling from her mouth. To this day, I have no idea whether it was pepper or ash that was in the mash.

Dinner started with a soup. The funny older brother's response after taking his first mouthful was, "Mum, this soup tastes like lukewarm piss!"

How I didn't spit out the tepid soup after hearing that, I have no idea. We might have been drinking Fanta with dinner, but as far as I was concerned that was champagne comedy.

Main course was steak Diane with peas and ashy mash.

Dessert was hot apple crumble with Peters Neapolitan ice cream. Talk about top shelf. And, just as the last dish hit the dishwasher, 'drungs' champagne comedy brother dropped another classic: "Sis, go to the shop and get me a packet of smokes, will ya? I'll shout you a bottle of Femfresh."

A bit like "tea", I had no idea what Femfresh was until Peta explained. Then I laughed till I almost wet myself. The following week I bought my own bottle — just in case of a future feminine emergency.

That's how puberty went. Bits of information and misinformation from everywhere — but you could always count on the sisterhood to set you straight…

Until you couldn't.

When I was twelve, one of my older girl cousins took me under her hairy pitted wing. When I say cousin, I mean it in the Greek sense: the daughter of someone who was married to someone who was vaguely related to someone who had baptised someone who was someone who someone knew… I think you get the drift.

There was an abundance of girl cousins in those days. I was one of the younger ones, and she was in her early twenties. She must have noticed the haunted, fearful look that all puberty ravaged teenagers get and decided to throw me a sweet, supportive bone.

My "cousin" and her fiancé would take me with them when they went to the movies or country drives or to picnics with groups of friends. She always did her best to make me feel included and a part of the sophisticated adult conversation.

Looking back, I suspect that I was her cover. In those days, Greek chicks weren't allowed to spend too much time alone with guys — even if they were engaged. And what better way to reassure the parents that there was no hanky panky (or, to use my mother called it, "the dirty bizzness") going on than taking a gawky teen with you everywhere you went? Still, she made me feel accepted, normal and, importantly, seen.

Then one day, she decided she saw too much. Or maybe her fiancé did.

We'd driven to the beach in Rye on the Mornington Peninsula — not to have a swim, it wasn't warm enough. Just a stroll along the foreshore, maybe get some fish and chips, just to get out of the city. I had my reservations about going to Rye because my body had betrayed me there once before.

Years earlier, at a family picnic, I had decided it was time Geoffrey (*Zaffiraki* in Greek) — my shy, inexperienced forever-indoors, hardly-ever-been-to-the-beach younger "cousin" slash neighbour — learned the ways of the bays. I considered myself a beach expert. As such, I came fully equipped: colourful beach towel, latest Dolly magazine, glamorous sunglasses, killer bikini — and most importantly Reef coconut oil for dependable third-degree burning. Or, as we liked to call it back then, "lobstering."

Geoffrey desperately needed some Vitamin D because, for a Greek, he was as pale as Feta cheese.

"Okay Geoffrey, let me talk you through how this works. I'll go first. Lay out the towel. Put the magazine on the towel. Lather body with coconut oil. Lie down on your back so you can keep an eye on the action. Bake front first until red hot and boiling. Then turn over, read the magazine, and bake the back. Once you've given yourself a good front and back frying, we go in for a dip to cool off. Then we do it all again and again. You with me?"

Geoffrey, as per usual, nodded his perplexed head and did as he was told.

Cut to: 20 minutes of deep frying later and we were ready to plunge. I stood, checked out who was watching me, and I ran into the sea, like a Bond girl in reverse, diving headfirst into the waves. When I surfaced, I realised I'd made a huge mistake. My body reacted instantly to the cold water. I don't need to explain the fight-or-flight instinct — so just say, as far as your bowels are concerned, there is no such thing as fight.

They panicked and evacuated like a building on fire.

Unfortunately, agreeable Geoffrey followed my instructions and was now approaching — oblivious to the fact that a brown floater the size of a Pepsi can was now bobbing between us. I had to act. Fast. I tried to splash it away, but every time I made any progress, Geoffrey splashed back, thinking we were playing a game. So there I was, one arm splashing him to keep him at bay, the other trying to send the 'Poopsi' out to sea. Somehow, that damning piece of disgusting evidence sailed off towards Bass Strait, sparing me a humiliation of epic proportions.

So with that incident burned into my memory, when my cousin and her fiancé suggested a stroll along the Rye foreshore, I was relieved we weren't planning a swim. None of us had bathers anyway. I was in shorts and my new white T-shirt, and I was staying in them. But then it got hotter. And hotter. And hotter. And the water looked so good.

Sensing what was on my mind, my cousin said, "Go on, have a swim."

"But. I haven't got any bathers."

"That's okay, go in in your clothes — they'll dry."

"Yeah," I thought, "They will."

This time, I eased myself in. No encore of the 'Poopsi' incident, thank you very much. The water was amazing. But after a while I got bored of being in there alone, so I headed back to my cousin and her fiancé on the picnic blanket.

As I approached, I noticed a strange look on his face. His eyes bulged, getting wider the closer I came. Was he having a stroke? Or had some kind of noxious sea creature latched onto my T-shirt? I looked down. There they were. The girls. The cha-chas. The ta-tas. Still young, budding and pert. Not fully surfaced, but enough to poke through a wet T-shirt and broadcast to everyone the exact temperature of the water. And my cousin's fiancé was staring at my chesticles like a crazed Titiologist — a sleazebag who studies the developing breasts of unsuspecting pubescent girls.

I was mortified. Then I saw my cousin's face. One look at him, one look at my chest, one look at me — and I knew, my ride-along days were over.

After that, my cousin found every excuse to avoid me. She'd say things to my mother like, "Watch out with Mary. She's a little more developed than she should be." Basically, implying that I was the problem. In other words, that I was some mega-mole in waiting. What? I'm not the one that was perving at a twelve-year old's chest. I couldn't help what my body was doing. I felt angry. But mostly disappointed. It wasn't the first time I'd been betrayed by a member of the sisterhood that should have known better. And it wouldn't be the last time I'd pay the price for something that was more about my body than me.

Over time it became blatantly obvious to me that females were easily swayed either by their own insecurities or the pressures of the patriarchy to undermine their own gender.

I loved being a girl, and I refused to let pathetic excuses and agendas that did not benefit me stop me from trusting girls and women. It did teach me a valuable lesson though: choose your pussy posse well. And I did. I chose them one by one. Based on their character, generosity, openness, intelligence, and humour.

Without them, I would never have escaped the fog of menopause — or found the drive to want to help other women through it.

"I don't think we should pash if it's over twenty-six degrees Celsius."

CHAPTER 13

THE PERFECT PASH

If there is any upside to my menopause 'journey,' it's that writing about it has caused me to look back on my physical life and demystify many experiences. There is, however, one mystery that endures — and I still can't quite understand — although I think climate change might be a significant aspect of it. It revolves around what we, in the Seventies, would refer to as a pash.

At high school, having a reputation as a "top pash" was the ultimate status symbol. Having blonde hair was a definite advantage for attracting the best-looking guys. Golden blonde hair that could be styled like Farrah Fawcett's in *Charlies Angels*, coupled with Roman sandals that laced up all the way to your knee — if you had those two things, and you could tongue-pash successfully, you were automatically in the upper echelons of the school social order.

Even though I never quite understood the allure of kissing, I knew it was an important first step on some kind of mysterious journey that I was supposed to take. A journey that would eventually lead me to the glorious joys of womanhood. Or something like that.

Like in that old movie that started my own private version of *Diary Of A Pre-teen Pregnancy*, the pash led to the couple walking through the door, staring lovingly into each other's eyes, the door closing, and the slow fade-out to… something. I didn't quite know exactly what then. I just knew it was something amazing, something important and something that set off a chemical reaction in my body that simultaneously felt good and scared the shit out of me.

So, while I was looking forward to my first pash, I knew that I had to be ready for what came after. And I also knew that if I didn't get it right, that would be it. There would be no "after," and no hairstyle, no footwear would save me. I'd forever be known as a "dud pash," and social death would follow. Luckily, I had access to one of the most legendary pashers in the history of the school.

My Estonian friend — yes, the active, forward, experienced one who had once eagerly offered to show me, step by step, bit by 'pink' bit, what her boyfriend had done to her friend — was, amongst other things, a pashing legend.

She was the undisputed suburban Doncaster queen of the pash and ruled the most vibrant social venue in our suburb: the local creek. (As well as a few other predictable locations.)

She was geographically elusive, forever disappearing with boys. Whenever anybody asked where she'd been, all she'd say she was, "Down at the creek." Sometimes she'd mix it up with four other words, "Down at the oval" or "Behind the shelter sheds," or even "Up at the shops."

Those four words said it all, so I never pushed her for details.

What I did know for sure was only bad things happened, "down at the creek" or "behind the shelter sheds." It was in there that her legendary pashing status was cemented.

I was reluctant to ask, "Got any spare pashing tips?" For fear that she might wanna do a live "Her lips on my hairy top lip" demonstration. She'd offered before, so she might very well offer again. Me? I wasn't interested in that option I just wanted to know what was involved.

Quietly, I'd been rehearsing in private with citrus fruits but I was unclear about of the tongue pace. How much should I inject? Should my tongue be stiff or flaccid, or maybe both? Should I be moving my head side to side? If so, how much and how often? And then there were the sounds. What sounds I should be making?

I did, however, feel confident about my hands. I figured my fingers would be busy running through their hair, so I wasn't worried about that.

With so much involved, I was in a quandary: how to get this vital intel from the only person I knew with the talent and reputation of an elite pasher.

Then it hit me: she loved food. I'd buy the information out of her. And where better to go for something tasty and exotic than the food court at Shoppo — our incredibly inventive Aussie nickname for Doncaster Shopping Town.

That weekend, I begged my mum for some money to go out to eat. Not easy. If you've ever tried to get money from a Greek mother to buy food prepared outside of the family home, you'll understand the emotional gymnastics required. Not only is it considered a personal insult that you'd even think of eating someone else's food, but you also you have to sit through a detailed cost breakdown of the meal and how much less she could make it for at home. In the end, I appealed to her racism.

My mother, like most Greek mothers, believes that anything outside a Greek kitchen is the Third World. She pitied my underfed friend, so she gave me the money.

With cash in hand, we headed to Shoppo for a mouth-watering beef and black bean with fried rice. The fried rice made the meal a little more expensive, but I figured it was worth it considering my possible pashing upgrade.

Between forkfuls of beef and rice, invaluable wisdom on the perfect pash was imparted. It boiled down to three areas –

Lip firmness — Too firm is uninviting, like you're forming an impenetrable barrier. The queen said, "You don't want to look like a Catholic virgin." However, too soft and you're inviting all sorts of mayhem. Just the right amount of pressure means you're open to suggestions, but you're also proactive if things get too whacky.

Moisture regulation — While you're not in total control of this, since there's another mouth and foreign saliva involved, you need to make sure to get rid of any excess personal saliva before going in for the lip-lock. Especially if you're kissing what the queen refers to as "wet-mouthed eager beavers." If you do encounter one of those, best to break off from the kiss, pull them in for a hug, and sneakily wipe your mouth on the shoulder of their shirt whilst pretending to nuzzle into their neck.

Tongue control –- As I suspected, one must combine both firmness and softness when pashing. But there are also other considerations: timing and point of entry, reciprocity of probing, circular as opposed to darting motions, and moisture content (see Moisture Regulation).

Armed with this information, I began training in earnest — with as many oranges as I could. When we ran out, I switched to the soft part of my arm between the forearm and bicep. After several sessions, I had what I thought was a solid lip technique and lively, intriguing tongue action — but was still having some issues with moisture.

I put this over-abundance of fluid down to my overheated Mediterranean blood. While I was sure the lucky guy I chose for my first pash would take that into account, I wished there was a little less spit involved. Little did I know that eventually, a whole desert would be waiting for me in the Meno years.

Within a couple of weeks, I decided I was ready. I felt my pashing had reached a level of professionalism that even the Estonian Pash Queen would be proud of. Now, all I needed was a victim… I mean, a co-pasher. And the perfect scenario.

This is how I had always envisioned my first kiss:

We're walking together, arms around each other's waists. It's a bit awkward staying in step, but it's worth it.

The sky is a brilliant blue hue with the odd cloud drifting by in the shape of something that makes us smile — like a large merino sheep, an old lady's hairdo, an oddly shaped penis. (Not that I'd seen a penis in person, but I'd seen boys doing drawing of them in class, so outline-wise I was up to speed.)

The longish grass is brushing against our flared Wrangler jeans — well, his Wranglers; I'm wearing Staggers Jeans (the fashion fanatic's choice) — making a rhythmic shushing sound that echoes the soft beating of our in-synch hearts.

On one side of us is a wild, beautiful vista; on the other is a chain-link cyclone fence — suburbia beyond it — and we travel along this path, between the savage and the civilized. In silence. In love.

Suddenly, he stops and pushes me up against the fence. My hair flicks back, my lips glisten with anticipation and moisture. There's a moment of panic as my back is pressed into the metal and I almost bounce off. But then his arms are around me, and I see his face, contorted with lust and need, and I succumb to my own passion.

But first, I must I distract him momentarily. "Is that a bat in that tree?"

His head turns. I wipe my saliva-filled mouth on my sleeve.

He turns back. I giggle foolishly, "It must have flown away."

Our mouths meet, clumsy at first — because for both of us, this is the first kiss — but then lips and tongues find the rhythm, dancing together, conveying all that we need each other to know about how we feel in this perfect moment.

Then I do the most erotic thing I can ever imagine. I slowly wrap my arms around him, reach down... and slip my hands in the back pockets of his jeans. So. Hot.

Before you ask, I have absolutely no idea where any of this came from. There is no scene like this in Change Of Habit, Saturday Night Fever or The Way We Were — my go-to movies for all sexual, dramatic and dance references.

All I know is that there were a few crucial elements needed to ensure the first kiss was perfect, and a chain-link fence and back pockets were the most important. Even more important than the guy.

In the end, I chose... well, let's call him Bobby. Not because that was his name but because he was from the most admired family in the street. Behind their backs we referred to them as 'the Kennedys'.

Bobby's sister was in my year at high school and the only girl more popular with the guys than the Estonian legend. Let's call her Marcia, because she had the special stink of The Brady Bunch all over. She wasn't loose or available she just... was. She was the type of girl boys fell in love with.

Marcia had all the things you needed to make it at high school (if you weren't prepared to put out at the creek, that is). She had the year-round perpetual tan, the feathered Farrah sun-kissed blonde hair, the Roman lace-up sandals, and she was absolutely symmetrically pretty in that particularly suburban Australian way. In fact, she was Queensland personified. As the old tourism ad slogan went: "Beautiful one day. Perfect the next."

Bobby was a year younger than both Marcia and me, and was just as popular and as pretty as his sister. His skin was completely acne-free — no mean feat for a twelve-year-old boy — and his Dunlop Volleys were a dazzling white, pure as driven snow.

Being a proto-cougar, I didn't mind that Bobby was younger. Despite the age gap, we still had plenty to talk about. I can't remember exactly what, but I'm sure we said something to each other in the two weeks we were together. And let's face it, I wasn't that interested in talking to Bobby. There was a whole other way I wanted to communicate with him.

Still, I put in the hours, walking around the school with him, holding hands or, in my preferred position, side by side with a hand in each other's back pockets.

Bobby, however, wasn't quite the proactive Casanova type that the boys down at the creek were. I started to wonder if he was ever going to make a move. After two weeks, as the cougar in the relationship, I realised that I would have to be the one to initiate things.

On the momentous day, we were walking home from school. There wasn't a chain-link fence in sight, so I decided the low brick fence of one of our neighbour's would have to do.

The first hitch was that I couldn't lean my back against it — let alone bounce off it when he threw me against it in a fit of passion. So, we both just sat down. Even then, Bobby missed the obvious clues and just stared at me blankly. So I leant in slowly, shut my eyes, and went for it. Lip firmness? Perfect. Moisture regulation? Check. Tongue? A few little slips. but for my first time — not too shabby.

When we finally broke off the kiss, I was ready for stage two: the "staring longingly into each other's eyes before having another even longer pash" stage. Instead, Bobby frowned and cleared his throat.

Then he said something I never expected hear — something I suspect has never been uttered before or since: "I don't think we should pash if it's over twenty-six degrees Celsius."

Uhhh, what? Hello?

Who has ever broken up over weather issues?

I was so confused by the reasoning. In my shocked state, I just agreed it was probably a good idea, and we walked home in silence. It wasn't until much later that I realised, "Hey, it's the end of November — summer starts in a week."

Doomed by the next few months of heat and the reality that it was never going to be less than twenty-six degrees except for those brief cool change moments, I came to the sad conclusion I had been absolutely, positively and literally dropped like a hot, desperate-to-pash, potato by Bobby Kennedy. Because of the weather?

To this day, I have no idea why. Did I have bad breath? B.O.? Was I too aggressive with the tongue?

Oh my god! Did I have wet-wog mouth? I tried so hard to keep that saliva under control. Or did Bobby just have some strange meteorological reaction triggered by heat?

As you may have guessed by now, I was used to my body turning on me, but I still don't know what exactly sent Bobby running for the Doncaster hills.

Yes, my body was hitting me with something new almost daily. New sensations, new bumps, new odours, new tufts of hair growing in new places.

But what the hell, Bobby? What happened, my little hottie?

It wasn't until years later, that I had my chance to ask Bobby why he dropped me when I bumped into him at the local branch of my mother's bank.

Before internet banking, if there was an issue with an account, you had to physically go into the bank and talk to a human being.

When I went in to clear up a problem to do with my mother's account, my human being turned out to be Bobby — working as a teller. Bobby was still pretty and still had vaguely the same hairstyle that he had at school — *Americana* meets *Eight Is Enough* meets Michelle Pfeiffer in *Scarface*.

I approached the window and his eyes lit up as he recognised me. By then, I was what my Greek Mother would refer to as a "Sumborry" — a person of note.

My career had been going well, and I was on television regularly as Effie — and maybe there was a Logie Award or something involved somewhere along the line, I really don't remember…

Bobby was delighted to see me and even more delighted that I remembered him. I explained what I needed to do regarding my mother's account, and he went off to fix it.

As he walked away from the window, I decided that when he came back, I was going to interrogate him about why he dumped me and what, if anything, it had to do with the bloody weather.

But as he moved further away, I caught sight of him full length and realised that his body had become very voluptuous in the intervening years — a shape that is usually attributed to women.

Maybe my body had turned on me that day on the fence, but Bobby's body had turned on him. Mr Perfect was now Mr Pear Shaped and, as a fellow victim of bodily betrayal, I couldn't help but feel sympathy for him.

By the time he got back to the window, I didn't have the heart to ask him anything about our breakup. Instead, I told him how great it was to see him again and I left. But not before asking how 'Marcia,' his sister was. Bobby answered enthusiastically, "She's managing the Dandenong Sizzler!"

And there you go: life is one big, fat, hot, awkward, heartbreaking smorgasbord of surprises.

I still don't know why 'Bobby' dumped me but I'm kind of glad he did. Seeing him all those years later was closure for the young me who didn't fit in, who rehearsed non-stop for love and lust but never even thought to rehearse for weather conditions.

I've learned a lot since then. That true heat isn't about weather — it's controlled by an internal thermostat called acceptance and self-love. And that's fuelled not by climate, but by whether or not you believe in yourself.

And if anyone has taught me more than any perfect Kennedy, or Estonian pashing Queen, it's the Queen of my making — the hairy, hot by nature, frigid by necessity, working-class Woggy Greek Goddess, Effie.

A character that's built from many of my childhood experiences and a legend that coined the phrase, "How Embarrassment" — the much-quoted, all-purpose, unapologetic phrase that reminds us of how embarrassing being human can often be.

Once hormones leave they're never coming back.

They haven't had a momentary tantrum.

They've packed their bags and driven off into the sunset forever.

CHAPTER 14

BE PREPARED

"But doctor, there's something wrong with me. I can't get out of bed in the morning, and I don't think it's my legs."

"Well, it must be in your head then. Please get up, we need the bed. It's an emergency. We have a male with an erectile dysfunction issue."

There I was lying in my bed, not knowing why I felt completely disabled by something I couldn't identify.

It must be me. What else could it be? I had a happy life. I finally had everything I needed and wanted, and yet…

And yet, every morning I'd wake up to an inner monologue that started with two words: "Oh God."

All because of hormones.

Here's what I now know about hormones: once they leave, they're never coming back. They're not having a momentary tantrum only to return. They've packed their bags and driven off into the sunset forever.

They don't rock up two years later and say, "It's been hell without me, hasn't it? Do you get it now, Mary? You can't live without me, can you?"

Like I said earlier, when I suggested to my doctor that I suspected my ten years of IVF might have masked the symptoms of perimenopause, she was starting to get the picture — but she was still a little annoyed.

I insisted on the blood test to confirm my suspicions. She reluctantly agreed. And by the time I left the office, I knew two things for sure: first, that I was definitely right about me and menopause; and second, that given her irritability, she was menopausal too.

A female doctor was reticent to give me a menopause diagnosis. How about that? She's lucky I didn't diagnose her before I left.

Two days later, the doctor rang:

"Mary, your estrogen and progesterone are at negligible levels."

"No shit, Sharon."

Of course, I didn't say that but I was tempted to ask her to make an appointment with herself and demand she give herself a blood test to check her own hormone levels.

Menopause is a chameleon. That's what makes it hard to recognise.

Menopausal symptoms mimic so many other things women have experienced throughout their life stages: from girlhood, to motherhood, to general-life pain-hood.

So it's easy — even logical — to mistake them for something we've had in the past, with hot flashes being the only thing that really screams "menopause." The rest of our symptoms scream silently into the echo chamber of familiarity or medical disregard.

"It's a fuss about nothing, it's in your head."

"It's not a big deal."

And yet, we are unnecessarily plagued with discomfort and, even worse, great suffering.

The Boy Scouts have a motto: "Be prepared." They're ready for all sorts of situations.

The knot, for example. They learn how to tie six different kinds of knots. Why? Because they're "prepared." They'll probably never need to use that knot-tying skill, but they have it just in case. Because that's what you do when you want to be prepared.

Yet we women, expected to prepare so much for everyone else — from schedules to school lunches and family dinners, and on and on — are somehow not prepared for a huge change that was always coming.

The Change.

The thing that ties us into six different knots.

Menopause.

I fell ignorantly into that category. And it cost me — and my ill-prepared, knotted body. I have always thought I was well across female issues, whether physical or social. But as you've probably guessed from some of the stories in this book, I tend to fall through the cracks sometimes. We all do.

Isolation — from others, from information, and from solutions — comes at a price. And the isolation is not just geographic — it's gendered, it's cultural, it's social, and sadly, it's medical.

If there's a personal blame game to play, then I blame Shame.

Shame isolates us more than anything. And shame is something most women are born with.

We become accustomed to it. We forget to question it. It plagues us. And more often than not, it forces us to take responsibility for things that we are in fact victims of. I would like to campaign for shame to take a redundancy package:

"Take the wins and walk away, Shame, knowing that you showed up every single day with a work ethic and a commitment like very few."

Shame's only competitor is Guilt.

Guilt, like Shame is relentlessly dedicated to the job of being a toxic wingman to most women. And Catholics.

"Guilt, please pack up your things, return your swipe card, and exit quietly along with Shame. Your disservices are no longer required."

Instead, we need enlightenment, information, support, and solutions. And we need to make a difference. We women need to take the power and to make those changes — because it's obviously not a priority for anyone else.

I spent a big part of my childhood listening to my dad's liberating words, "Don't expect anyone to make your dreams come true. That's your job"

His philosophy dictated so many of my decisions throughout my life, that I started to think about that idea in terms of my nightmares — our nightmares.

Be Prepared

"Don't expect anyone to wake you up from your nightmares. That's your job."

Gender was something my father was blissfully blind to. He rated people by their character only. He saw that as the dictator of all outcomes. He knew strength came as a result of personal integrity, not physical capacity.

He didn't focus on the obstacles, only the opportunities that they came with.

He saw the ambitious girl in my mother — now a wife and mother herself — and he encouraged that ambition in her. He persuaded her to take driving lessons in the early 70's when we knew of no migrant women in our social circle that drove. He wanted her to have her licence and more independence.

He opened her mind to the cultural offerings of Asian cuisine by taking her out to Chinese and Indian restaurants when none of our family friends had interest or opportunity to do that themselves.

He socialised with her and his Danish and English work colleagues and friends so she could mix with people of different ethnicities. And she loved it.

Her English improved and her confidence grew. He constantly empowered her to go beyond the easy and familiar.

That was how he loved. That was his gift to us. He saw what was possible for each of us, and with him as our champion, we saw it too.

He bought me a typewriter at seven so I could write. And then, when I graduated from acting school, he urged me to tell my story — our stories — and I did.

That changed everything.

It allowed me artistic autonomy. It gave me the confidence to control my own narrative and to contribute to a cultural landscape that, up until that point, was in a diversity deficit.

And in doing so, I claimed my place — not just as a storyteller, but as proof that our voices, our lives and our cultures belong at the centre of the story.

Finding my comic and creative tribe in actors Nick Giannopoulos, Simon Palomares, and George Kapiniaris — who, like me, were looking to impact and entertain at the same time — was a massive game changer.

Wogs Out of Work and *Acropolis Now* were cultural awakenings for so many Australians who were searching for characters and stories that represented the world they lived in.

They needed to be seen — and so did we.

That typewriter is long gone, but I am still compelled to write every day. To tell my story. To be seen. Because there's power in that.

Sometimes I wonder how long I would have endured the depression of the back hole I found myself in, if I hadn't demanded those blood tests.

From a female doctor!

Fortunately, things are changing in the medical profession as women have exercised their power and started demanding to be seen.

And why can't we make demands of the people around us? Especially when we're sweating, shivering, itching, and bloating — because a bunch of hormones have fled our bodies.

And especially when those same people make so many demands on us…

The elephant in the room of most long-term couples is a lack of sex.

It's what brought us together and what ultimately might tear us apart.

CHAPTER 15

APPLES, ORANGES AND DEAR DAIRY

I don't want to get into the differences between men and women again but… yes, yes, I do.

I don't consider myself a pessimist, but the gender war will never be resolved. We just don't look at things the same way. And men don't look at all.

When my daughter Jamie was in preschool, they would do 'Show and Tell'. One week, during the "tell" bit Jamie in one simple sentence, revealed the difference between what men see and what women see in our household: "My dada loses his wallet twice a week but my mumma always finds it."

There's no arguing with the fact that we see things differently. And because of that, we argue. We argue because we want to believe we're right, which must mean the other person, must be wrong.

I think women are as ambitious as men.

Men (generally) are vertically ambitious, and women (generally) are horizontally ambitious — and that is in no way a sexual reference. Most men can afford to be single-minded with the objective to look ahead and forge ahead.

Meanwhile, most women look panoramically across a spectrum of things with the objective of moving forward horizontally.

We multi-task and multi achieve because we have to. Even in a household where both partners work, the day-to-day business of living is never completely split 50/50.

A male friend once said, "Men are in a sit-com, and women are in a movie."

The idea is that men live for the moment, happy to hit reset and repeat the experience next week. Women, however, live a continuous narrative where every moment and detail has meaning, and the story never ends — it just twists, turns, and becomes richer, leading to a deeply satisfying outcome.

At the core of this — let's face it — flawed observation is the expectation that women do the 'small stuff' so that they can come back and enjoy it.

As if to say: "Details? That's the woman's job."

As I said, men want women to stay exactly as they found them, and women want to renovate men. I read recently that men try to change women's feelings while women try to change men's behaviour.

Men: "Don't ever change, you're perfect as you are."

Women: "If we could just fix his wardrobe…his friends…his family… his lack of ambition…his drinking…"

Also, men collect facts while women collect feelings. This is never more obvious than when men and women argue.

Men: "When did I do that? What exactly did I say?"

Women: "You always do it. You do it all the time. It's not even what you say. It's how you say it."

I can't even remember how many times George has said to me, "You're comparing apples to oranges."

Me: "Apples to oranges? I'm trying to give you a context. I'm trying to get you to connect the dots. Can you see the dots? Or are the apples and oranges in the way?"

While great relationships demand hard work, I've confessed in moments of frustration, "I wish I was a lesbian! A relationship with a woman would be far more efficient." Then I remember the Estonia Queen and her eagerness to digitally demonstrate her sexual shenanigans on me quickly reminds me — maybe I should have learned about my own equipment from a master of her own

A bit like owning an Apple laptop and taking it to the Apple Store Genius Bar in order to find out how to get it to do what you want. The relief you feel when you walk out satisfied that you are a little closer to being a genius yourself.

Women feel exhausted by having to do more than they should, a lot of the time. And men are exhausted by trying to understand women.

A bestie once asked me on one of our many regular walks, "What's a normal amount when it comes to sex?"

My answer was, "I don't know what's normal. But I know what's not normal. Not normal is not having it."

The elephant in the room for most long-term couples is a lack of sex. It's what brought us together and yet has the power to ultimately tear us apart. For some, this is a tragic loss of intimacy, while for others, it's a welcome relief from expectation. Some couples break up because of it, while others stay together for the companionship — the kids, the mutual friends, the life they built.

It's a bit like supporting a team that never gets to the finals. It doesn't mean you stop barracking for them, but you lose hope that you'll ever get the cup again.

I get it. I support Collingwood in the AFL and my husband is an NRL Rabbitohs supporter. And there were many years — decades even — of cup drought.

But you stay committed because of those amazing high-scoring glory days in the start. Then, out of nowhere, a rare phenomenon strikes, like Halley's Comet — and you're back on top!

Months after Jamie was born, George said something that stopped me cold, mostly because it was so inarguable:

"I suspect my parents are having more sex than we are."

And I suspected he was right. Could my 83-year-old father-in-law and my 78-year-old mother in-law — who don't even like each other, by the way — really be having more sex than my husband and I? Who, by the way, I actually adore?

It's hard to argue with the facts, so I didn't. I got back on that horse. I remembered how to ride that bike. And the work bench was back in regular use.

It was a much-needed pattern interrupt. And we all need those.

A friend, a year after giving birth to her daughter was trying to get her body back to it's pre-pregnancy state. She had tried watching what she ate, exercising and giving it time, but she wasn't making much progress.

One day she optimistically put on her favourite pre-pregnancy jeans and came out of the bedroom in tears. Her male partner, confused, asked, "What's wrong?"

She stood there, her jeans zipper wide open with no hope of it being done up.

"My jeans don't fit! I've tried so hard and they don't fit. See?"

His response? "Just get a bigger pair of jeans."

She stormed out and called me, sobbing,

"He just doesn't get it! I know I can get bigger jeans, but I don't want bigger jeans. I want to fit into those jeans."

She didn't end up buying a bigger size. Instead, eight months later, she was back in her favourite jeans, and the ugly miscommunication of "Jeangate" remained unaddressed.

It seems some men find working things out exhausting — especially if a woman will do it for them.

"Does it hurt to think, Georgie? You'd rather exhaust me with a million questions than think for yourself? Is that it?"

"I figured you'd know, so I asked you."

"George, you have a Maserati parked in your upstairs garage. Please take it out for a spin every now and again."

The thing is, I see George thinking often. But it seems he only wants to think about what he wants to think about. I'll often find him deep in thought, assuming it's about something of great significance.

"Georgie, what are you thinking about right now?"

"The footy."

I suppose that's significant — especially if you think large men pushing and shoving each other often from behind, to get a ball over a line is a good use of great intelligence.

Yes, there are so many delightful differences between men and women — and we overlook, accept, or embrace every little peccadillo.

But, then menopause hits and, as I've already established, those peccadilloes become motives for justifiable Georgicide.

Without a doubt, George is getting more eccentric as time goes on, and more creative. But not in the ways you would expect. As I mentioned, he's been a brilliant advertising Creative Director for decades, but his creativity doesn't stop there. No, George is also quite the creative director when it comes to his consumption of dairy products. His maternal grandfather in Greece was an exceptional cheese maker, and as a result, George's lifelong love affair with dairy seems, somehow, genetic.

George knows no limits when it comes to goat milk — or should I say milks. Yes, he's a polygamist when it comes to milk. The more milks, the better. And he loves a cream too. The guy has enormous range. He's the Meryl Streep of dairy.

My father-in-law, Mr Jim (as I affectionately call him), coined the brilliant and much-quoted phrase amongst our friends: "You can't have a party without cheese!"

I can certainly confirm George can't have a pizza party without cheese — and lots of it. If we go out for Italian and there's a four-cheese pizza on the menu, you can guarantee George will order it and ask for a fifth. True story.

Look, I find it impossible to judge the guy because I know where he came from. It wasn't just the influence of his mother's dairy-farming side of the family. It came from his father's side too. George has genetically found himself trapped in a vice of lactose.

I know. I know. I hear you saying, just look away. But I can't. Not when the estrogen is fleeing and the progesterone — a vital contributor to our ability to feel empathetic towards others — is gone. Knowing that your husband's ideal state is to be sleeping peacefully in a bathtub brimming with assorted milks is infuriating.

Come to think of it, I'm really starting to question the origin of the bovine related nickname "Mou"...

Despite all the George jokes and references to his eccentricities — his nightly NASA-like sleeping preparation rituals, his over-the-top lactose-loving ways, his bulge-phobia, his love of multiples, his repeating of things I heard the first time, his endless losing of things that aren't lost but he just can't find, and his ability to be conveniently Oblivia Newton-John about anything onerous for me and tedious for him — I know are all exacerbated by menopause.

Everything is exacerbated by menopause.

Things that used to be cute and comical can so easily become frustrating and infuriating. Menopause can be a profound exclamation mark on things that we would in the past have been considered a "no biggie."

Before I knew it was menopause I felt like I was living in the movie, *The Quiet Place*, isolated and constantly retreating in silence while my body filled with anxiety.

On other occasions, it reminded me of the hilarious heavy metal mockumentary, *This is Spinal Tap* when the guitarist Nigel Tufnel refers to his amplifier and says, "It goes to eleven."

Menopause pushed me to eleven at times.

And there were plenty of days when I felt like Ron Burgundy (Will Ferrell) in the comedy film *Anchorman*. In one scene while losing his mind in a telephone booth, Ron is asked by Paul Rudd's character Brian Fantana, "Where are you?" The overwrought and hysterical, tear-filled Ron replies, screaming, "I'm in a glass cage of emotion!!!"

I've felt like that in peak moments of menopause.

I like my wine dry.
Not my vagina.

CHAPTER 16

THE SHOW MUST GO ON

I know that, by now, I've well and truly established how blindsided I was by menopause and how late I was to act. Since finding out a lot about it — and finally getting the hormonal support I needed in the form of MHT — I feel so much better.

It's made a huge difference to me. And so did being able to talk about it with friends and family. All of which brought me back to my favourite form of therapy, writing. Incessantly writing about it has helped me discover all the reasons why it went the way that it did.

Most of them, you've encountered in this book — misinformation, no information, a propensity to blame myself, a sense of shame, bafflement, confusion, a past fraught with tragedies and missteps, and a propensity to ignore the signs my body was giving me.

Some of these things may seem more familiar than others. But the one thing all women share — and will identify with — is this: even more basic than no information, no motivation, no communication is no time.

This is not a book of advice. It's a book that hopes to give you some relief.

Comic relief. To make you laugh a little.

But if there's one thing I would love you to do (besides be heard, be seen, get the treatment you need, learn more, etc.) it's this — write out what you did today. And how you felt. Then do it again tomorrow. And I don't mean a list of the highlights; I mean get forensic with it.

If you've been blindsided by menopause, if you're feeling guilt or shame for not realising it sooner, then the best way to let yourself off the hook is to sit down and actually come to terms with what you have to do every day. And it's a lot. Too much, many would say.

Who knows? You may even find a way to pass some of the tasks off to your dairy-obsessed, sleep-dedicated, "I don't need a set of car keys to give me a bulge," hunk of manliness husband.

Or you may decide to do less for others and more for you.

Whatever you choose, please make sure you pat yourself on that heroic back of yours for always stepping up and doing what had to be done — against all odds, with a body that was depleted but definitely not defeated.

Here is an atypically busy menopausal day. A crazy-busy day where, like many others, I was guilty of not finding the time for me to do that.

I'm exhausted just reading it. Granted, there were some fun and funny bits and some great peeps that made all the difference.

One Frazzled Friday:

2:03 am — Dread lets out a sound, "nawwgghh." I tell myself, "Just get cosy and go back to sleep." But it's pointless.

The panic of not getting back to sleep has taken over. At least since MHT there are no heart palpitations. Unlike the Stanley Kubrick film, my eyes are wide open.

For the next hour — I stare at the ceiling, check the alarm and run through my to-do list of deadlines: publicity call, Today show… Try to sleep, but it's not happening

3.25am — Go to the bathroom. Check clothes in the dryer to see if Jamie's uniform is dry. It's not. Put it back on. Head back into bed, get comfortable. Sleep.

4.47am — Eyes spring open again. "Please, I gotta get another hour under my belt." The sleepy part of me is trying to lure the awake part into sleeping. Eventually, the sleepy part wins.

5:52am — Eight minutes before the alarm, I'm awake.

I get out of bed and, like a drunk, stumble into the kitchen. Put the kettle on. Go into recess and lunch making mode. Pull everything I need out of the fridge and dry goods from the pantry. The kettle boils. Place boiling water into a small saucepan, add salt, and once it's boiling, add penne pasta for Jamie's lunch. Heat up my pre-made bolognese in another small saucepan. Cut up fruit. Chop capsicum and cucumber. Place Sicilian green olives and small bocconcini into tiny containers, together with a packet of popcorn, a seaweed sachet, and a small bit of dark mint chocolate Kit Kat. Place hot pasta and sauce into a thermos and top with parmesan. Fill the Stanley bottle with filtered water, and I'm done.

6.45am — Try to wake up Jamie.

6.46am — Jump in the shower. Quick 4-min shower. Teeth brushed, moisturised, and dressed. Boobs feel a bit sore. That said, they look pretty good. Thanks, Meno.

6.56am — Ask Jamie to get up again. Jamie gets up. She showers.

7.00am — Get clothes out of the dryer. Lay out her uniform. One day formal. One day sports. Another day's polo shirt and skirt. Occasionally mufti.

7.03am — Lay out polo with skirt. Wrong uniform. Formal today — white shirt and tie, navy tights, navy skirt, and blazer.

7.05am — Make her breakfast — a hot chocolate and a piece of toast because she needs to leave room for the seven-course meal at lunch and recess.

7.10am — Get Effie ready — wig, dress, accessories, stilettos. Book an Uber.

7.30am — Yell out (nicely) for George to get up.

7.32am — Email Jamie's teacher about an early afternoon school pickup. She has a dental appointment.

7.35am — George emerges, saying, "What does Jamie have on today? Choir, netball, drama??"

"Drama. She has everything she needs. I have to head to Channel 9. See you. (Quick kiss) I gotta go."

Put the Effie gear in the Effie roller bag and head out the door.

7.40am — Jump in Uber.

8.00am - 10.00am — Brief the makeup person on Effie's look, "More Kardashian than Drag Queen." Get dressed. Put on hairs, jewels, heels, and accent. Do the interview. Plug tour. Crack jokes. Do photos. Say goodbyes. Get changed. Book Uber.

10.05am — Jump in Uber, head home. Tired already, and it's only 10am.

10.15am — Effie interview with Adelaide radio station. Uber driver is amused.

10.35am — Home. Check emails. Put on coffee. Need to do Effie video to promote the tour on socials. Get back into her clothes and wig. Why did I take them off?? Hasselhoff. Drink coffee. Shoot video. Nailed it.

11.00am — Doorbell buzzes. The 'specialist' smoke alarm guy arrives to check the alarm. This job requires a complex piece of equipment: a broomstick. That's why they get paid the big bucks. He's perplexed as to why Effie has answered the door. 'Specialist' pushes broomstick towards the ceiling, hits the smoke alarm bullseye button, the alarm sounds, and he's out the door within 45 seconds. Legend.

11.10am — Shower again. Wash off makeup. Get into something comfortable.

11.25am — Late breakfast and hit the computer for an hour and a bit — to do some writing for an upcoming corporate job in Brisbane.

12.45pm — Jump in car to pick up Jamie from school to take her to the dentist. Dull headache. Bad thanks. Guzzle a 500ml water; hopefully that'll fix it.

1.30pm — Jamie dentist. Weirdly, unlike most kids, mine thankfully likes the dentist. No drama except for the credit card hammering. She needs a retainer. Ouch. Possible braces in the next couple of years. Dentist hopeful that the retainer fixes the problem.

3.00pm — Drop Jamie home. I have an hour before having to jump in the car again to drive to tonight's venue for a 5pm sound check. Google maps indicate that it's 45 mins away. I have to give it at least an hour. I haven't done this venue before, and it's Friday afternoon, so the traffic is going to be ugly.

4.00pm Jump in car. Drive out west.

5.00pm — Arrive at venue. Tech person's name on worksheet is John. See a man behind the tech desk, smile –

"Hi John, I'm Mary"

"Hi Mary, I'm Doug. John's not on tonight and we have a problem."

"Already?"

"Yep. The computer's on the stage and I'm back of the room. Also, the lights are controlled from the right-hand side behind the curtain. I'm the only one that's on tonight. So, I can't be in three places at once."

I really want to say, "Der Fred". Instead, I say,

"Yeah, that is a problem."

Doug continues, "Also…"

Me, "Also??" Shoot me now.

Doug, "Yep. We've been having problems with the laptop. I dunno what's up with it."

I take a deep breath,

"Any good news by any chance, Doug?"

"Nup. None of this is my fault."

I try to crack a joke. "Is it John's? Is that why he's not here?"

"Mate, I don't know. All I know is the equipment's old and it's stuffed."

5.03pm — The RSL manager enters the room,

"Hi Mary, I'm Wendy. Everything alright?"

A bit like Doug, Wendy would've preferred I just said, "Everything's great." But I didn't. Because it wasn't.

My heart's now racing. Is it meno? Or am I just worried the show's going to be a technical disaster?

Wendy springs into action,

"There's a young girl who's a tech wiz who works here. Let me try to find her."

5.13pm — Wendy's back with the knockout tech wiz woman. Late 20's, flaming red hair and arms full of tattoos. She's all over it. I hand her my USB stick, and she's pressing laptop keys non-stop, like a stenographer in a court case.

Standing next to Wendy is a middle-aged, sweet-looking guy called Darrel.

Darrel usually works on the floor collecting glasses, but he can help.

He looks terrified. Darrel didn't need this pressure in his life. He needs to turn up, pick up glasses, and go home. Instead, he's looking like a soldier about to be sent into a war zone.

5.18pm — Gun tech woman has the video on the screen, she guides him through it over and over again until there's some colour back in Darrel's terrified face.

Me? Headache's back. Worse. More water and a couple of Panadol for insurance.

Meanwhile, all Doug has to do from the comfort of his padded high stool is sit on his arse and make sure the microphone is on. And loud enough.

While poor Darrel battles with the laptop, the lights, and the nervous breakdown he's having.

5.45pm — Support act arrives to check microphone. Darrel heads off to have dinner and no doubt a stiff drink.

Overworked Doug suffers through two minutes of "check one, check two. Checking one two, one two," and sound check is over. Doug can relax now (for a change).

6.30pm — Dinner. A chicken parma and a salmon fillet arrive backstage.

There's a bottle of wine in the bar fridge, and at this point, I'm contemplating sculling the whole thing. It's a crisp sauvignon blanc. Meno Mary's thinking: "I like my wine dry. Not my vagina."

7.30pm — Doors open.

8.00pm — Support act on stage.

8.30pm — Support act finishes.

9.00pm — Effie hits the stage.

The audience is so brilliant. Up for everything. The laughs are huge.

And the 25-minute improvisation in the second half of the show is beyond. They give me gold.

For that entire hour, everything is paused except for the pure joy we give each other.

I look at Darrel, who's only meters away, and he's having the time of his life. And Doug, of course, at the back of the room looking down at his phone.

After the show, I get into the car and, with adrenaline still coursing in my veins, I make my way down the freeway, relieved, happy and grateful for the gift that Effie is to me and her fans. To the incredible audiences that I have, that give me more than I can grasp.

11.20pm — Arrive home, unpack my things.

11.35pm — Jump into the shower to wash off, in the words of Effie, "the heaps and heaps of makeups," and the huge day that was.

11.45 — Take MHT: a swipe of estrogen and a progesterone capsule down the gob. All good.

11.50pm — Curl into bed. George wants to know everything. I tell him about AWOL John, slack Doug the 'technical guy' and the shitty set-up, the quick thinking Wendy, the superstar flame-haired redhead laptop legend, and of course the biggest star of all — glass-collecting Darrel, who literally peaked in front of my eyes. And of course, the audience, who was beyond epic. I'm wrecked. Time to sleep. I pray I can sleep through…but if the sleeping data over the last few years is anything to go by, I don't fancy my chances.

2.17am — Eyes open, "Nooooo not again…"

Okay, so, my days aren't often typical, but I think you get the point. Not a lot of time to think about what I might need. I felt stretched, sore, and spent through most of it, even though there were some great laughs amongst all of that.

But you know what they say, and it applies to us forever-juggling women as well as those in show business: "The show must go on."

Misinformation
and fear have for
years buried positive
menopause information.

Like a dog hides
a pig's ear.

You're lucky
to find it tucked behind
a couch cushion.

CHAPTER 17

SEVEN PERCENT

Some conversations can change the course of our habits and stagnant thinking. They are much-needed pattern interrupters.

Left to our own devices, we can easily fall into autopilot, flying over the same psychological terrain again and again. Most of us want to believe we have all the answers, but we don't. As uncomfortable as it can be, there's nothing like some loving, radical honesty to help us get closer to where we want to be.

I am eternally grateful to the people in my life who loved me enough to have the hard conversations with me — conversations motivated by a desire to guide me away from my nightmares and closer to my dreams. That's the healthiest love. That's the gift of great love.

It's the gift I give to my daughter, Jamie, whenever I can. And it's the gift I wish I could have shared with my daughter Stevie, who was stillborn so many years ago.

Our conversations are far-ranging, sometimes nonsensical, but always filled with love and sharing. Ultimately, I want Jamie to know more than I did — and also to know less: less shame, less guilt, less fear.

Unlike my mother, I didn't want to wait until my daughter was in her late thirties before dispensing any advice. I always answer every question as honestly, humorously, and — when the occasion demands it — as graphically as necessary.

Jamie, like me, has had her moments of considerable hair concerns. Once, as I was waiting to take her to a friend's party, she came in and announced she didn't want to go. I asked her why, and discovered the socially self-conscious chick gene had kicked in already.

"Mumma, my legs have a lot of hair on them. I don't like it. It doesn't look nice with my dress."

Me? I'd been there, shaved that.

"It's okay, my darling — I can help."

Relieved and teary, she smiled.

"Can you, Mumma? Can you help me? Can you fix it for me?"

"Yes, I can. Absolutely I can."

And off to the bathroom we went to look for her dad's razor — just like I looked for my dad's all those decades earlier.

Every gender knows their touchy, triggering, "don't risk the wrong type of attention because of this" rules.

I believe it's our job as parents to let our kids know of the potential social land mines up ahead. We wish that somebody had told us ahead of time — but for many of my generation, as I've amply explored elsewhere in this book, this was not the case.

And I don't really blame my mother. For her generation, it was even worse. No conversations about anything vaguely adult, physical, or sexual were ever had. Ever. Maybe that's why my mother didn't have them with me.

I would never want generational awkwardness to stop me from preparing my kid for what's up ahead. Outsourcing parenting to Google or YouTube in modern times isn't an option. Plus, they lack the humour to make the icky bits stick.

A bit of humour or a clever joke is the perfect combination for dealing with hard topics. It makes the embarrassing, awkward pill easier to swallow. It makes it easier to remember, more quotable, and reminds us how funny it is to be human — even when so many of the things that happen to us were never designed to be funny.

"Mumma, why does Dada have an elephant trunk down there?"

Whaaaat? That's talking it up!

"Elephant trunk?" I tried not to laugh. "Darling, that wiener is called a penis. Boys have a penis, and girls have a vagina."

My confidence in this area was not only because I had gone through it myself, but because I'd had those conversations before with Nathalie.

Just over three decades ago, our family and hearts 'unofficially' adopted a little girl we all fell in love with. Nathalie was 10 months old, and her parents were living two doors away from where my brother and I were lived in the early nineties.

My mother was emerging from years of mourning my father's death. After eleven heart attacks, the man with the cotton-wool face who had always urged us to get out into the world and make our own stories finally gave up the race on a day when he had two major heart attacks within hours of each other.

My mum spent the next few years lost, and then suddenly blossomed. As she tells it, my father came to her in a dream and beckoned her to join him. Instead, she told him she had more to do, that she was living for her family now, and she wasn't finished yet. With the same spirit she showed at the age of seventeen when she left the fields behind, she kick-started her life for the third time. And to her already humongous strength and courage she added a sense of humour and spontaneity.

It was in a spontaneous moment that she asked Nathalie's parents if they needed any help with their baby, not for money, but because my mum had the time. Both Nathalie's parents were high-achieving professionals and were grateful for the offer. Nathalie was part of the family.

Nathalie is now in her 30's and one of my greatest loves. Over the decades, Nathalie and I have had every hilarious, uncomfortable conversation you could possibly imagine — and some you probably couldn't.

I remember talking to her when she was younger about a man's 'favourite elephant trunk slash wiener.'

"Nat, I just want to prepare you for the shock of when you see a penis for the first time. My initial response was pity. Pity for the person who had to walk around attached to that bizarre-looking thing. My second response was: there's no way I'm touching it."

It's not just the male body parts that lacked a little design-finesse.

Years later, I again asked Nathalie, "Nat, have you ever bent over and had a good look at what's happening back there?"

She enthusiastically admitted she had. Her response: "It's a lot."

Relieved that she's done the physiological research, I continued.

"It is a lot. And it's not pretty either. Maybe that's why it's hidden back there. I feel bad for it. It's camouflaged itself, knowing very well it's not a good-looking feature. I admire the renovators who go to great pains to bleach it, hoping to increase its kerbside appeal."

The body is a funny thing — penises are funny, boobs are funny, balls are funny. I don't really know about labia or flaps, but I reckon they might be funny too.

Farts are funny — but only when they're yours.

The body is funny…until it's not.

Until it doesn't deliver what you need it to… or what you never expected.

Like when you're a little girl going to a party and your legs are a little too hairy.

That's when I am happy to pay it forward and give whatever advice or perspective I can. Even if it's as simple as: "Get me the Remington."

And even though I firmly believe in the idea that your body is your business, women can't help but get into each other's business regularly — physical and emotional.

"We can't fix most problems alone. That's why we reach out to people who can help. We seek out those who want the best for us and who see the best in us — people we trust like family, friends, teachers, and professionals. Our job is to ask for help, and it's our job to offer it in return."

"Have you ever asked for help, Mumma?"

"Yes, I have. When Mumma was really sad, after Stevie died, I knew I needed someone to help me with all the hard bits, so it could be easier. I needed someone I could talk to. Someone who would understand. Someone who could help give me the tools, so then I could help myself. And, Monkey, that made a big difference: it helped so much. We're not in this world alone. We don't need to solve our problems on our own. Please don't forget that."

"Okay, I won't forget… Mumma, can you help me open this popcorn packet?"

Not exactly what I meant about reaching out for help, but we've got to start somewhere. I guess popcorn might be a good beginning.

And as much as I'd love to tell her she can do anything and that she doesn't need to rely on anyone but herself, I know that's not true. What I desperately want Jamie to know is that no matter how capable she is, we all need help.

When things get heavy, we need help with the lifting.

When things get complicated, we need help with the untangling.

And when we don't have the answers, we have to find them.

I'd love to tell her she's the smartest girl in the world and that her Mumma is 'Mensa Mary.' But we aren't. And if there's one thing I know for sure, it's that if you think you're the smartest person in the room, chances are you're not.

The memoir I wrote when Stevie died was called *All I Know*, named after the Greek philosopher Socrates' profound quote: *"All I know is I know nothing."*

This title reflected how limited my understanding of life before Stevie's death was compared to the profound realisations I made afterwards.

Socrates, despite being one of the world's greatest minds, humbly recognised the importance of acknowledging what we don't know, viewing it as the true path to wisdom.

The title also reflected the fact that I never feel like I know enough.

I know now that I didn't know nearly enough about menopause. In fact, I might not have known anything at all.

What I knew was that your period finishes and that you might get hot flashes. A bit like inheritance tax — you'd rather not know the negatives to a positive. So, I put off knowing about it. But it didn't put off knowing about me.

No, it moved in stealth-like, throwing me a little off-kilter every now and again. And slowly getting rid of things. Like a jealous girlfriend who rips up photos of her new boyfriend's ex. Or a controlling partner who deletes people from your contacts list.

Before you know it, you start losing touch with so much of what you were accustomed to: sleep, libido, metabolism, memory, patience — and eventually yourself. And you start to think it's just time wearing you down.

You contemplate bringing it up in conversation to see if you get a bite from a bestie — or five. Only to realise most of your girlfriends have already eaten and digested the meal that is menopause. And the few that haven't are so in denial they're not even hungry. So, it's just you left sitting there with nothing but the carcass of a chook to bite on and the washing up to do.

Thanks to the flawed findings of the *Women's Health Initiative* in 2002, misinformation and fear have for years buried positive menopause information. Like a dog hides a pig's ear. You're lucky to find it tucked behind a couch cushion.

So, you dig further and start looking everywhere, waiting for confirmation from the right source — which at this stage is me and some social media influencers — to officially verify me as an overdue and overdrawn member of the menopause association, otherwise known as the parched pussy posse.

If information is power, then the power is way too often in the wrong hands. So, you look for reliable, healthy, and informed sources and become your own private medical insurer and advocate. And before you know it, you're meeting more and more women who have been misdiagnosed, overlooked, and abandoned by medicine.

Only 7% of medical research is dedicated to health issues that impact women.

How can that be? That is unfathomable. That is inhumane.

I am — we women are — that statistic.

We are the casualties of that number, of that dereliction of duty. And yet we are the ones that birth, raise, and nurture daily.

We work, we wash, we cook, we clean, and sometimes we may even have sex (but only if it's not a total fire ban because, with a dry menopausal vagina, too much friction and not enough downstairs pubic back-burning, you could start a small fire).

Still, what we do is not enough. Not enough to be valued to the same degree as males. Not enough for our health to be worth investing in. Just not enough.

And yet women live longer than men. Women generally live between five and seven years longer than men. Finally, a gender gap that's in women's favour!

Unfortunately, according to a global health gap analysis, the research also suggests that women experience more years in poor health, including a higher burden of non-fatal conditions like chronic pain and mental health issues.

The experts say that there is an urgent need for action to boost women's health.

No joke, Johnny.

"Oh God, how am I going to get out of bed?"

"Oh God, why is my chest aching?"

"Oh God, I hope it's not my heart!"

You try not to overindulge the fear, so you give yourself some tough love. "Mary, if it was a heart attack you wouldn't be having this conversation now. Just get up and get on with it."

I take a deep breath, and I get my sorry arse, sore chest, and sunken spirit up and out of bed.

It's a Sunday, so it's 'God's Day' and I should feel good about having acknowledged his/her presence multiple times already.

And because it's Sunday, it's a day of rest, right?

Are we victims
of a hit-and-run?

Actually, it's
a hit-and-sit.

And the culprit is my
83-year-old mother-in-law.

CHAPTER 18

THE HIT AND SIT INCIDENT

It's Sunday, so it's Jamie's sport first up, then maybe some writing, followed by the main event — my in-laws coming over.

I prefer them coming to ours for many reasons:

A. They live 45-60 mins away — that's almost 2 hours in the car; with all due respect, I'll pass!

B. They're old, and they deserve to dress up and get out.

C. I don't need my mother in-law to drag every piece of crystal glassware out of her cupboard and fill the table with so much food that there's no room for the plates — or the crystal glassware.

D. I like to cook.

Jamie's basketball was a basket case. The opposing team had the wrong game time, so the game was forfeited, which meant Jamie's team won on paper. Great, more winning for doing nothing.

Which sort of falls into the category of getting a trophy for 'participating,' which is a politically correct word for 'turning up,' 'losing,' or 'breathing'. Yep, that's really preparing our kids for the real world!

In any case, with that waste of time behind us, we were back home where George and I hit the kitchen to prepare lunch. George is an experimenter — he's not monogamous to a recipe — so there's a lot of, "I'm thinking of adding some…" or, some "I'm gonna try something different this time."

I make the point that Subway isn't Myway or Yourway — it's Subway.

McDonalds isn't McDougalls or McWhatevers — it's McDonalds.

These brands are built on consistency, on delivering what people expect and like. The Colonel didn't screw around with his eleven herbs and spices. People don't turn up to the counter and ask for three less herbs and four more spices. Okay, maybe George would, but no-one else does.

I made what I believed to be my inarguable point, and I left Donna Hay — aka George Betsis — in the 'test' kitchen to continue experimenting.

Meanwhile, I try to ignore the loud banging pots, kitchen cupboard doors opening and closing, and the endless chop-chop-chop sounds, and focus on writing.

I even try to block out the, "Mumma, can you…? Mumma, where is…? Mumma, what time…?"

And the occasional barking dog, trying to justify its free rent and utilities deal by pretending to protect us from intruders — or in-laws.

Every sound is loud, every interruption unnecessary, and everything is agitating me. And the weighted feeling I woke up with is still swamping me.

The phone rings. George answers. It's my father-in-law, Mr Jim and my mother-in-law, Tina. They're downstairs in the garage and need help with the parking.

"Mou, could you...? I just need to finish up here?"

Mr Jim, who's 89 at this point, and Tina, 83, are waiting in the car.

Tina sees me. "Hello, Mary."

"Hello, Teens, hi there, Mr Jim. Tina, why don't you jump out, and I'll park the car? I'll reverse it back in."

Tina replies, "Yes, good idea. Thank you, Mary."

They open the doors. Mr Jim grabs his walking stick and slowly gets out. I stand at the driver's side, door open, waiting for Tina.

Here's when things get a bit hairy.

Tina, who for the record your honour is a very good driver is sadly not one today. For some unknown reason she's left the gear stick in Reverse. Instead of Park.

Stepping out, she accidentally pressed her foot on the accelerator, which makes the car lurch back in reverse, taking down both Mr Jim and I. We are both knocked down by the open doors. Bang!

We hit the concrete floor at the same time, with full-bodied falls.

"Sorry, God, I know it's supposed to be your day off, but we appear to be victims of a hit-and-run. Well, more like a hit-and-sit. And the culprit is my 83 year old mother-in-law — with an otherwise flawless driving record."

I look under the car and see one of my favourite people in the world, my father-in-law, Mr Jim and his walking stick sprawled out like a sack of Greek potatoes.

I get up, a bit sore, but nothing broken. I bolt around to pick up Mr Jim.

"Mr Jim! Are you alright?"

The champion replies, "I'm alright, Mary."

I pull him up onto his feet, pick up his walking stick, and walk him to a safe area.

I couldn't help myself: "Mr Jim, Tina nearly knocked both of us off at the same time. Win-win. Daily double."

He laughs.

"Can't get rid of us that easy, Mary. Tina's usually a good driver."

Meanwhile, Tina's blaming the car: "I… I don't know what happened. I put it in park…"

I said, "Are you sure it's in Park now?"

"Yes, it is, Mary."

"We're okay, by the way. Thanks for asking."

I look at Mr Jim and he's laughing.

Tina, still confused, snaps back to her priorities: "Mary after you park, can you please grab the banana box from the back? I've brought some feta, olives, and fresh spanakopita I made this morning."

"Can do Teens — that's if my arm still works."

She ignores the reference to the hit-and-sit incident as well as the joke.

"Thank you, Mary."

They head for the lift, my father-in-law still laughing and shaking his head with disbelief.

The morning had started with a bang — literally.

I already felt like I'd been run over, flattened by a menopausal Mack truck when I woke up, only to find myself literally run over by a Mazda 3. Not quite as dramatic, but definitely funnier.

That's when it dawned on me, my mother-in-law had hit me with more than a car — she'd hit me with the truth.

I can survive this.

If I can be knocked over by a car and serve lunch five minutes later, I could endure the rest of it: the dryness, the lack of sleep, the anxiety.

I was getting support, the MHT was starting to work, the communication in our house was improving, and I survived a hit and sit.

I'd say that I turned a corner, but I just hope Tina's not behind the wheel as I turn it.

But at least I began to understand that I was going to be good… thanks.

Hormones are King.

And Elvis has left
the building.

CHAPTER 19

HAVE OVARIES? WILL MENOPAUSE

A male friend, years ago, asked me randomly, "What do you know?" My reply was, "I think I've noticed plenty." His response wasn't what I was expecting, "That's not good. Because you can't forget what you know." I thought that was pretty philosophical — especially coming from an Italian.

I've never forgotten that comment even though, since menopause, I've forgotten a lot.

In my funny, sometimes scary, and often humiliating physical life, I have discovered much about myself — and a lot about the female body and the power and powerlessness it evokes in us women. It offers us such incredible pleasure and yet it contains so much debilitating pain.

This anatomical enigma demands we listen to it, trust it, and take care of it. I paid the price for not listening — and for not knowing nearly enough to know what I was listening for.

I had no true understanding of the immense role of hormones. But I do now.

My simplest way of explaining menopause to someone who knows nothing about it is:

Hormones are king. And Elvis has left the building.

They're our body's Uber Eats — they deliver what we need.

Honestly, would Jeff Bezos be one of the richest men in the world if Amazon didn't deliver? No, he wouldn't.

The other thing I know for sure, from these last few years, is: being mute when something's not right is the highest form of personal negligence. It only aids and abets pain.

Yes, I was in a fog, but I would have come out of it so much sooner if I'd just talked about it. But I didn't. And yet I tell my daughter regularly, "Problems are there to be solved. Most problems we can't solve on our own. That's why we're not alone. You ask for help, because that's how you get it."

I didn't take my own advice — and I paid the price.

I never want my daughter to suffer unnecessarily like I did. I want her to make healthy, informed choices. And I want her to understand what's ahead for her physically: to be prepared.

I want that for every girl and woman.

Here's the other thing I know, I am not a doctor. And even though I'm an actress, I've never played a doctor. But I have had a lot of experience with them. I have been lucky enough — especially throughout my IVF journey and during my pregnancies — to have been in the care of some magnificent ones. I have shouted gleefully from the rooftops to anyone and everyone about these medical maestros who made my 'almost' impossible dream come true.

IVF is not for the faint-hearted. Like menopause, it can be hormonal hell. But if you can withstand the cost of that hell — physically, emotionally, and financially — then sometimes, hopefully, a lot of the time, you can get what you desperately want.

Menopause, unlike IVF, is an inevitable stage for all women. Finding those medical maestros to help us navigate the hormonal ups and downs during menopause is the mission.

Making it easy and accessible for women who are doing it unnecessarily hard is the goal. And placing those doctors somewhere convenient for any woman in Australia to depend on for their health is the dream.

That is why UnPause, our online tele-health platform, was created together with those amazing women you met earlier. Our goal is to help every woman, regardless of postcode, manage her menopause

Or as Effie would say,

"Ladies, c'mon… I don't know about youse, but I'm over the whelm! I'm all for Dry July — but Dry August, Dry September, Dry October, Dry November? Enough already! It's time for the parched pussy posse to get hormonally hydrated."

EFFIELOGUE

GOOD THANKS

Effie is the character most associated with my career as a comedy performer. She began life on the sit-com *Acropolis Now* as a seemingly vacuous, self-absorbed airhead — who was such an intelligent, charming manipulator that she always got what she wanted. Back then, all she ever wanted was for Ricky to love her, a VIP badge for the mythical Vibrations Disco, and money for 'heaps and heaps of make-ups'.

By the time the show ended, I felt I was just discovering some of Effie's hidden depths, so I kept on digging. In the ensuing years, she became a celebration of everything ethnic, working class, female, and a bold outsider — all those brick walls my mother was afraid I'd crash into. Effie not only made them acceptable, but she also became a very loud, enduring voice, not only in comedy but in the cultural life of the country.

I often speak professionally at corporate functions on subjects from race to resilience, to gender, to being the underdog (or underwog in my case). I love it because it's a challenge I relish. I've performed for banks, telcos, venture capitalists, corporate leaders, real estate agent associations, vegetable growers, and insurance industry guns — the list goes on.

It's a look inside industries outsiders rarely see. I research each client extensively and then place Effie at the centre of their world. I find out who's who, what they do, then write a monologue weaving it all into a bespoke show for their awards night, yearly celebration, or conference.

Here's the thing: when professionals gather in a conference room overflowing with food and booze, it's an amphitheatre of anti-theatre. They're there to network and talk. Effie's job is to make them listen.

Effie is a high-haired, high-status, ballsy chick who's not accustomed to taking rubbish from anyone.

She demands the room's complete attention — and she gets it.

Fear of public humiliation is her weapon of choice. Nobody wants to be singled out by a sassy, fast-thinking, sharp-tongued Effie.

I'm regularly invited to speak at women's events. Whether it's high-flying professional ladies, diverse community or charity groups, or young girls, I like to reinvest in the gender pool that I am so grateful for.

This multitude of women love drinking from the female, cup-filling, spiritual, communal chalice. They want to rehydrate their womanly optimism — and who better than a self-made, working-class, Logie Award-winning Greek goddess like Effie?

Exactly.

Effie prefers to have these women drunk on laughter than alcohol.

I performed the monologue, below, at an International Women's Day function a few years ago. Effie was invited to speak alongside some big female guns. The speaker before Effie was a highly accomplished and lauded public figure who delivered many speeches. Her husband, a retired lawyer, was with her.

Guilt is a common issue for women. We feel it too easily and far too regularly.

Guilt was obviously present when the successful 'gun' woman hit the stage. No doubt, because she's had a far more visible career than her husband, Kevin.

And everyone knew it — including Kevin.

Halfway through her incredible speech, she went off script and somehow it became all about Kevin. She started spruiking just how brilliant Kevin was, how wonderful his career had been, and how he had so many skills she could only wish for.

As if that wasn't enough, she decided to invite him on stage to say a few spontaneous words.

Kevin wasn't prepared, and neither were we. But it didn't stop him.

And so a room full of women, at their annual function, were held captive by Kevin, talking glowingly about himself.

Effie was visibly perplexed, along with everybody else in that room.

Kevin's proudly uninspired speech ended anticlimactically. And after some token, lukewarm clapping, he strutted back to the official table.

The only one smiling, nay beaming, was his even prouder wife.

Then Effie was up next. The host introduced her, and with enthusiastic applause, Effie and her up-itself ego made their way to the stage.

"No please don't. Don't. Stop. Please don't stop! Happy International Women's Day, ladies. Before I go on, I just wanted to quickly say: Kevin, a quick question. Are 364 days a year not enough for you, mate?"

Huge laughter erupted as she made a very fair point.

No further eye contact was made, however — with either Kevin or his somewhat embarrassed, guilt-ridden, legend of a wife.

Comedy enables us to laugh at the undeniable, often unspoken truth. And Effie has always voiced her self-evident truth, not only on behalf of the room, but on behalf of an entire country.

I wrote this book to offer relief, reframe some language and norms, and hopefully deliver some laughs as well about a heavy subject.

But I'll now hand it over to the outspoken hairdresser/goddess to give us some further inspiration.

Effie, please?

"Yes, thank youse, Mary.

"Hello, good thanks, ladies.

"It's a great pleasure to be with all of you magnificent women here today. Well, I'm here to help raise hairs, standards and spirits via the currency of laughter.

"I am here today because the sisterhood called, and I never say no to that call. This is a special occasion because it's the first time many of youse would have seen me in person.

"I know what youse are thinking, 'She's even more beautiful in real life than she is on screen' and it's true.

"But the truth is: you can't judge a book by its cover. Trust me, I've bought a lot of books with covers, only to find nothing but writing on the inside.

"I, Effie, have always played by my rules. I have refused to suck up, play down or apologise for who I am, and because of that, I stand here tonight as a cultural phenomenon that's had to 'bitch-fight' her way to the top.

"Life is dog-eat-dog. And it's obvious I'm no vegetarian.

"Some people say I'm up-myself, and my response to that is: 'So what if I am?'

"Loving yourself isn't vanity, it's sanity.' You have to be up-yourself. You have to celebrate who you are… and, in my case, it's a never-ending party.

"Today is a day of celebrating us and youse.

"Ladies, we women are unbelievable. I love women. I must confess, I am physically heterosexual, but I'm psychologically homosexual.

"In my life, I have been called many things: wog, megastar, Logie award winner, cultural icon, and modest. Okay, maybe not modest.

"Look at me: I'm charismatic, attractive and popular. I could go on — but why rub it in?

Good Thanks

"Like youse, I have: many dimensions. Many contradictions. Many flaws — as if.

"Being flawed is what being human is all about. We're not produced on a factory assembly line where we all come out perfect and the same. Okay, I came out perfect, but youse get my drift.

"Yes — I Effie, am many things, but mostly I am woman. W-o-o-m-a-n.

"And however stunning I am on the outside, it's actually what's inside that's even more impressive.

"My personality and my spirit are supermodels. But I, Effie, do not 'only rely' on God's great work, because the truth is: since birth, I have been working nonstop on the behind-the-scenes of me, building my esteems,

"Defining myself according to: what I think of me. And because I have been so abundantly blessed, I want to help change the perceptions of how people view: ballsy, passionate, outspoken and way too often unrepresented women like me and us.

"It is my mission to put and keep women on the map — always and forever.

"Yes, that's the responsibility that comes with being a legend, a woman, a legendary woman.

"But I am not alone with this legendary status because in this room tonight and in every room where women are gathered, there are:

"Ladies, legends, leaders. Girls, girlfriends, goddesses. Mothers, miracle workers, mind readers. Jugglers, juggernauts, job holders. Hand-holders, man-holders, and soul soldiers.

"My God, how good are we women?

"Let me tell you, ladies, youse are both the chicken and the egg. Yes, youse are everything, and everything is youse.

"We need to celebrate our epic efforts, our individual differences and to find comfort and awe in our collective same-ness-ness.

"Ladies, think of me as your 'hairy' fairy godmother. Yes, I am here to remind you of all that you are and all that you can be.

"In order for us women to rise to the heights of our infinite potential, we need to change. We chicks need to be up-ourselves. We need to love ourselves. We need to stand up for ourselves, and we need to speak up for ourselves.

"We need to be proud of our efforts, our gender, our culture, our originality, our vision and our impact.

"We need to be unapologetic about our 'strengths' and honest about our insecurities.

"We need to guide and support. Inspire and mentor.

"We need to prop and be propped.

"We need to show and be shown.

"The truth is, there is nothing we can't do.

"Decades ago, women burned their bras — and even though I am very pro-feminism, I am very, very, 'pro-bra.'

"As far as I'm concerned, we women need to be each other's bras. We need to: support and uplift each other so we can be pert and upright.

"We need to make each other look good. Hello?

"We know and we see what women are capable of, and it's astounding and breathtaking. Every day is like running a marathon.

"It's incredible how much we can achieve — from the mundane to the miraculous. I have no doubt that men see that too.

"The truth is, us women must be intimidating to them. Of course, we are, look at us: we're powerful, able, dexterous and hot.

"We're tougher, stronger, and more resilient. Forget this 'quiet achievers' thing that might work for BP, but it doesn't work for youse and me. We chicks need to be loud achievers, proud achievers.

"We can no longer be apologetic 'under-the-radar' achievers. If we want things to change, then we have to change things. And things have to change.

"My greatest inspiration comes from every day ordinary women — not famous women

"And when I say 'ordinary' women, I mean:

"Women who are not advantaged by money, class or the influence of those with power.

"Instead, I mean fearless, phenomenal women who rely heavily on their own character in order to do something incredible. Women who touch our hearts and lives every day. Nurses, administrative workers, hairdressers. Ordinary women who do extraordinary things.

"They nurture. They help educate. They motivate, and they cut, colour, and blow-dry. They care a lot, and they do a lot.

"These women are our mothers, our daughters, our co-workers, our neighbours and our friends. And these women come in all shapes, sizes and colours.

"They are young, and they are old, and, in my case, they are age-less, and time-less.

"They are youse, and they are me. And, in the words of Annie Lennox and Aretha Franklin, these are, sisters doing it for themselves, and for us.

"You know these women. You were born from them. And you are them.

"We know it takes a village to raise a child. So youse can only imagine what it takes to raise a phenomenon.

"I should know. I am one.

"I'll tell you what it took. It took a phenomenal village of women. And they come in every flavour, every colour and every spice. And those tasty women are everywhere.

"So, on behalf of me — past, current, and future me's — I say thank youse. I love youse.

"And I thank God, the Universe, and Mother Nature for youse.

"Good bye and good luck, lady legends.

"And if I don't get to see you face to face, I'll see you in your dreams!"

THE STRAIGHT-TALKING GUIDE TO MENOPAUSE

Edited by
Dr Natasha Andreadis

UnPause Medical Doctor, Gynaecologist,
Fertility Specialist and Reproductive Endocrinologist
MBBS MMED FRANZCOG CREI INHC

Written by
Cheryl Fitzell

Disclaimer

The content provided is for general education to help you better understand perimenopause and menopause.

It's not a replacement for personalised medical advice, diagnosis or treatment from a qualified healthcare professional.

Please speak directly with a healthcare provider about your specific needs.

CONTENTS

About Dr Natasha Andreadis	186
A Few More Words from Mary…	187
Welcome to the Midlife Collision	188
What's Happening to Me?	189
The First Signs of Perimenopause	191
Is It Perimenopause or Burnout? (The Quiz)	193
Your Hormones, Explained Simply (Promise)	195
Perimenopausal Periods — When You No Longer Know Aunt Flo	197
Early or Premature Menopause — What You Need to Know	199
Menopause at Work: How to Survive, Thrive and Not Lose Yourself, Your Mind and Your Job	201
Mental Health and Menopause	203
Sex and The Pauses: Your Body, Your Rules	205
The Midlife Body: What's Changing and What You Can Do About It	207
The Power of Lifestyle Medicine — Movement, Food, Sleep, and Sanity	210
The Inside Skinny on Menopausal Hormone Therapy (MHT)	212

Alternative and Natural Therapies	214
Creating Your Midlife Support Team — Why You Shouldn't Do This Alone	217
Menopause and Men — A Partner's Guide	220
How to Talk to Your GP and Get Taken Seriously	222
Red Flags and When to Seek Help	225
Thriving Post-Menopause — Your Golden Age	227
Summary Cheat Sheet	229
A Note to Younger Women — Because This Is for You, Too	231
About UnPause — Your Midlife Menopause Concierge	233
Final words from Mary	234

ABOUT DR NATASHA ANDREADIS
UnPause Medical Advisor
Medical Doctor, Podcaster, Community Builder

Medicine and healing were my calling. After completing training in Obstetrics and Gynaecology, I underwent further subspecialty training in reproductive medicine and infertility (CREI). During this hard slog, I had the option of working a regular surgical list Monday mornings to further my skills in laparoscopic surgery or attend a menopause clinic. I chose menopause, mainly because after a full decade of medical training, I felt I still had very little knowledge and confidence in managing this phase in a woman's life.

Fast forward 15 years and menopause is a big feature of my private practice. It is also one of the most satisfying aspects of my work as a doctor, as I can see that when women are heard and cared for during the menopause transition, their lives change for the better. Not only their lives, but their partners', children's, friends' and probably even their pets' lives! Menopause management has a real-time ripple effect and I'm here to play a positive role in the changing of the tides for all my sisters out there.

Let's do this together!

A FEW MORE WORDS FROM MARY...

Menopause can be overwhelming. And we're over the whelm!

Putting the information you need in one place to make it easier was the objective.

Dr Natasha Andreadis is a talented, fun and passionate menopause advocate who's spent decades being dedicated to women's health.

You dream of doctors that understand women's bodies and needs. And then you find the incredible Dr Tash.

Mary and Dr Tash

SECTION 1

WELCOME TO THE MIDLIFE COLLISION

Puberty, pregnancy, childbirth, breast-feeding, and then The Pauses (peri, meno, and post); all of these are life changing. But at each of these stages, so many of us have apologised for our femaleness. We've hidden our bleeding (please God, make the pain of the stain go away). Said sorry when milk seeped through our work shirt and now (in what is arguably the prime of our lives) we regularly excuse ourselves from polite company until the hot flush passes, and return when we are professionally 'acceptable' and socially 'decent' , i.e., sexless. It's hard being a woman sometimes. It's a lot to bear. We know because we're women too. The struggle and the stigma need to ease.

It's called the midlife collision for good reason

Menopause isn't just that your hormones are crashing and burning. It's that everything else is, too.

- Holding down demanding jobs while feeling like you're living in a pressure cooker.
- Managing children and caring for elderly parents.
- Dealing with relationships that are suddenly strained.
- Wondering what happened to your energy, libido, and joy.
- Doing all of the above while thinking that you're going mad.

This is the midlife collision. And it's exhausting. It's not in your head. It's in your body, your chemistry, your brain, your hormones. And so many parts of your life.

The good news is this doesn't have to be a breakdown. It can be a breakthrough. With the right knowledge and support, this can be the beginning of your best chapter. That's not optimism — it's accuracy.

SECTION 2

WHAT'S HAPPENING TO ME?

The Three Stages of Menopause (aka The Pauses)

Menopause is just one part of a bigger hormonal story — a long arc of change driven by the slow decline of estrogen, progesterone and testosterone. These hormones influence everything from mood and sleep to bone density and brain function. So, when they start to drop, you feel it.

Here's how the stages unfold.

- **Perimenopause**

    This is the real main event. Your periods start to misbehave — showing up early, late, or not at all — while symptoms like hot flushes, brain fog, sleep disruption and mood swings quietly move in and unpack. Perimenopause usually begins in your 40s (sometimes earlier), and it can last anywhere from one year to more than a decade. Most women sit somewhere between four and six years.

- **Menopause**

    You're officially in menopause when you've gone 12 consecutive months without a period. Just one day on the calendar, technically — but it marks the end of your reproductive years. The average age? Around 51, but it varies. It doesn't mean everything suddenly settles. It just means you've crossed the threshold.

- **Post-menopause**

    The cycle is over. That said, your body's still adjusting. And the reality is those hormones are not coming back. Estrogen levels remain low, and that can impact everything from bone and heart health to memory, muscles and mood. This is the time to get more serious about long-term wellbeing — because you've got decades of living still to do.

Why Doesn't Anyone Understand?

Unless they're 'in it', most people don't 'get it'. Children? Clueless. Partners? Often sympathetic but baffled. Friends who aren't there yet? Trying. Colleagues? Well… Some doctors still wave it away as 'stress' or toss you a script for antidepressants. Don't you LOVE it when that happens?

For years, women were told to just get on with it. But that's not good enough anymore.

You deserve answers — and proper support. Not dismissal. Not confusion. And definitely not platitudes.

SECTION 3

THE FIRST SIGNS OF PERIMENOPAUSE

Perimenopause doesn't always make a dramatic entrance. No sirens, no flashing lights — only a handful of sneaky symptoms that leave you wondering; is it just me? (Newsflash: it's not just you. **It's us.**)

Here's what the early signs can look like.

Your periods are all over the shop

Once upon a time, your cycle ran like clockwork. Now it's ghosting you, turning up early, or arriving like it's got something to prove. Totally normal. Totally annoying.

Hot flushes and night sweats

The stars of the show. You're fine one minute, then boom — internal bonfire. Night sweats? Same deal, just with bonus sleep deprivation.

Sleep's a nightmare

Falling asleep takes longer. Staying asleep feels optional. And that lovely 3 a.m. wide-awake window? Happens to a lot of us.

Mood swings

One minute you're fine, the next you're bawling or furious over the smallest thing. Your dipping serotonin and dopamine levels are the culprits.

Brain fog

Can't remember that word? Or why you opened the fridge? Or why you walked into a room? Or where your phone is (it's in your hand)? You're not losing the plot, you're losing estrogen.

Everything bugs you

The sun is shining. Damn it, the sun isn't shining. Your husband's breathing has you contemplating murder! Your tolerance is shot because your progesterone levels are falling.

Skin and hair go off-script

Where'd this pimple come from? Why's my skin so flaky and itchy? Dear God, am I going bald? Why am I growing whiskers!? When estrogen dips, things get weird.

Downstairs drama

Vaginal dryness, discomfort, leaks or more frequent UTIs — it's either a desert or a flood zone and it's not climate change it's hormone change. It's not glamorous but it is common. And yes, there are ways to sort it out.

Libido's left the building

Testosterone's going bye-bye. Add dryness and fatigue into the mix, and intimacy slips wayyyy down the priority list. That's okay. You're not broken — you're recalibrating.

Your waistline's had enough

The kilos are sneaking onto your midriff and your gut's bloating for no good reason. Your metabolism's slowing, and estrogen is shifting fat storage. Cortisol (your stress hormone) isn't helping, either.

Achy breaky body

Back twinges. Joint stiffness. Estrogen used to help keep inflammation at bay. With less of it, your body's letting you know.

Teeth and gum tantrums

Bleeding gums? Wobbly tooth? Losing teeth? Turns out, estrogen supports bone density in your jaw, too. Of course it does…

Dry everything

Dry eyes. Itchy skin. Tingling hands and feet. Estrogen's moisture magic is fading, leaving you parched in odd spots.

Heart flutters and head spins

Palpitations, dizziness or headaches can be part of this phase, too. Often harmless, but always worth checking out.

SECTION 4

IS IT PERIMENOPAUSE OR BURNOUT? (THE QUIZ)

Burnout is real — work, kids, endless to-do lists — but so is perimenopause. And it can make everything feel ten times harder. The difference? Burnout eases with rest; perimenopause keeps putting pressure on your system until you tackle the hormones.

This quiz will help you work out where you're at. If you're ticking a lot of boxes, it's time to chat to a menopause expert.

Score 1 Point Per 'Yes'

Cycle chaos

- Are your periods playing hide and seek — early, late, or AWOL?
- Had a couple of no-shows this year with no explanation?
- Is it a trickle one month, a flood the next?

Body breakdown

- Waking up at Witching Hour (1–4 a.m.) for no good reason?
- Hot flushes hitting like a summer scorcher?
- Packing on kilos despite no change in habits?
- Joints moaning like you've done a CrossFit sesh?
- Skin or hair acting like it's auditioning for a horror flick?
- Bloated more often than not?

Mind meltdown

- Forgetting names, dates, or why you're holding a fork?
- Anxiety crashing your party?
- Crying at ads for pet food or car insurance?

- Snapping at people for existing?
- Feeling like your spark's gone walkabout?

Intimacy implosion

- Is sex about as appealing as a tax return?
- Dryness or soreness downstairs making you wince?
- Avoiding the bedroom like it's a crime scene?

YOUR SCORE

- **0–5**: Might be burnout or early days. Keep an eye on it.
- **6–10**: Could be perimenopause sneaking in — worth a chat with your doc.
- **11+**: Hello, perimenopause! Let's get you some help, stat.

To get clarity on your symptoms, speak to a doctor.

SECTION 5

YOUR HORMONES, EXPLAINED SIMPLY (PROMISE)

Hormones are your body's messengers. Right now, they're sending some mixed signals. Here's the simple version of who's who in the menopause zoo.

- **Estrogen: the multitasker**

    Estrogen's the queen bee—running your periods, keeping your skin plump, and helping your brain stay sharp. In perimenopause, she starts flaking out—sometimes high, sometimes low—causing hot flushes, mood swings, and that foggy head. When she's gone for good, your bones and heart need extra TLC.

- **Progesterone: the chill pill**

    This one's your calm-down hormone. It balances estrogen, helps you sleep, and keeps your womb in check. As it dips, you might feel wired, anxious, or wake up at stupid o'clock.

- **Testosterone: the fire starter**

    Yep, women have it too! It fuels energy, muscle strength, and that frisky feeling. When it drops, your get-up-and-go gets up and leaves, and your libido might ghost you.

- **Cortisol: the stress mess**

    Not a sex hormone, but a big player. Made by your adrenals, cortisol spikes with stress—and menopause loves to crank it up. Too much means more belly fat, crap sleep, and a shorter fuse.

How They Work Together

These hormones are like a finely tuned quartet — when they're in sync, you hum along with energy, focus, and emotional balance. But in perimenopause, the harmony starts to wobble.

Estrogen and progesterone usually work as a pair: estrogen energises while progesterone soothes. When estrogen spikes erratically (as it often does in perimenopause) and progesterone quietly declines, you get all the heat, tension and emotional whiplash with none of the calm.

Meanwhile, testosterone — your quiet achiever — adds spark, strength and sex drive, but it also tapers off, leaving you flatter and more fatigued. Then cortisol joins the chaos: when stress is high and sleep is low, this hormone floods your system, throwing your metabolism, mood, and patience completely off balance.

This new hormonal interplay hits your whole system. Understanding it means you can fight back with diet, exercise, or even MHT if it's your vibe.

SECTION 6

PERIMENOPAUSAL PERIODS – WHEN YOU NO LONGER KNOW AUNT FLO

Perimenopause turns your once-predictable cycle into a game of roulette — except the stakes are your underwear, your iron levels, and your patience. Suddenly, you're bleeding every 21 days, then nothing for 40. When your period does show up, it can hit like a crime scene. Other times? Just a vague threat and some bloating. Let's break it down.

Here's What You Might Notice

Flooding: The kind of bleeding that laughs in the face of regular tampons. Stock up on super-absorbents, reusable period undies, or a menstrual cup. Don't wait to be caught out. Think waterproof mattress protector. Think backup pants.

Random spotting: Light bleeding between cycles can be normal during perimenopause. But if it continues into post-menopause (i.e., after 12 months period-free), definitely get it checked.

Phantom periods: You feel the cramps. You're moody. You're bloated. But… nothing. Your body's trying to ovulate, or at least pretending to, without much success. It's messing with your head. Spectacularly.

How to Stay (Relatively) Sane

Track your symptoms: Even if your period doesn't play by the rules, having a record helps spot patterns — or lack thereof. Apps can help, but so can a simple wall calendar and a decent pen.

Check your iron levels: Heavy bleeding can drain your iron stores, making you feel foggy, flat, and exhausted. A blood test will tell you where you're at — and iron supplements (or infusions) can help.

Pain relief: Medication, heat packs, and gentle movement (even a walk around the block) can ease cramps. Yoga works wonders too — not the bendy Instagram kind, just the kind where you breathe and don't swear at your uterus. Strength and resistance training — now is the time!

When to Speak to a Medical Expert

- Bleeding that lasts longer than a week
- Soaking through pads or tampons hourly
- Clots bigger than a 50-cent coin
- Any bleeding after menopause
- Any bleeding that is unusual for you

Dealing with the emotional ramifications

Letting go of your period can feel like losing an old frenemy. Some women cheer. Some grieve. Most feel a bit of both. However you feel, it's valid. Talk to someone who understands.

It's not glamorous. It's not easy. But it is a rite of passage. And it needs to be managed. And with help it can be.

SECTION 7

EARLY OR PREMATURE MENOPAUSE – WHAT YOU NEED TO KNOW

Premature menopause is when a woman's final period happens before she turns 40. Early menopause is when a woman's final period occurs between 40 and 45. Up to 8% of women have had their final period by the time they're 45. The symptoms are often the same as perimenopause (hot flushes, mood swings, brain fog), but the timing can throw you. You're not where you thought you'd be and your body's doing things you didn't plan for — which can feel confronting, frustrating, and yes, a little unfair. But it's not the end of the road. Far from it. With the right care, support and information, premature and early menopause can be managed — not just medically, but emotionally too. This is your body taking a different path, and we're here to walk it with you.

Why It Happens

Natural: Your ovaries clock off early — it's genetics, pure and simple.

Surgical: Hysterectomy or ovary removal (oophorectomy) fast-tracks it.

Medical: Chemo, radiation, or autoimmune conditions can shut things down.

Toxins: Smoking cigarettes causes our ovaries to shut down sooner.

What It Feels Like

Same symptoms as perimenopause — hot flushes, mood swings, dryness etc — plus, the shock of "this shouldn't be happening yet."

Fertility's often off the table, too. It's an emotional reality that can hit hard.

Health Risks

Losing estrogen early ups your risk of osteoporosis, heart disease, and dementia. Not to scare you — just to arm you.

What to Do

See a medical professional: Blood tests (FSH levels) can confirm it. Don't let them brush you off with all that "you're too young" nonsense.

Have the MHT chat: Menopausal hormone therapy (MHT) can replace what's missing, easing symptoms and protecting long-term health. It's safe for the majority of women. Get the facts, not the (many) fictions.

Lifestyle: Weight-bearing exercise (walking, weights) for bones. Cut smoking and booze for your heart.

Get support: Early menopause can feel isolating. Talk to a menopause expert that can help you navigate the changes and ease the symptoms with the treatment that is best for you.

SECTION 8

MENOPAUSE AT WORK: HOW TO SURVIVE, THRIVE AND NOT LOSE YOURSELF, YOUR MIND AND YOUR JOB

We excuse our flushed faces, step out of meetings to ride out the 'sweats', then return once we've blotted, breathed, and re-assembled ourselves into something 'professional'. And just when the sweating eases, brain fog rolls in — names vanish, stats evaporate, and that killer phrase you definitely rehearsed yesterday is now hiding behind a filing cabinet. While we're at it, don't even get us started on the mood swings! Welcome to menopause at work — where you're expected to lead, deliver, and keep your cool while your hormones are holding your dignity hostage.

Enough.

Here's the good news, you're not losing your mind, you're losing your hormones. And you need help, space, support and solutions.

Viva la Flush (and Fog)

No more shrinking. No more silent exits. No more pretending you're the problem.

If anyone's uncomfortable, hand them a fan and a sticky note labelled 'Empathy' and get on with general business and the business of being you.

What Actually Helps

Cool it down: Layers are your best friend. Keep a desk fan handy. Drink icy water like it's a job.

Write. It. Down.: Lists, notes, Post-its, whiteboards, phone reminders — give your unpredictable memory the helping hand it deserves.

Take five: A quick walk. A loo break. A power cry in the car. Whatever resets the system.

Ask for flexibility: A simple, "Hey, I'm going through menopause, can I have a few more WFH days?" can open surprising doors. HR's heard worse.

It's time to Push for Better. It's Time for Positive Change.

Menopause is a workplace issue that belongs in the workplace conversation. Some companies have introduced menopause policies, so some progress is clearly being made. But we need more. If you think your workplace needs to become more menopause-aware, you can make a start by sharing this guide with your manager or HR department. You can also introduce them to experts like Menopause Friendly Australia who provide workplace training and accreditation.

And remember, you have a lot on your overflowing plate. It's a smorgasbord of demands and expectations. You don't have to take on that extra shift or organise the team trivia night. Cut yourself some slack. You're not failing, you're doing brilliantly under conditions that would make a lesser mortal cry. If Man Flu is unbearable could you imagine what Menopause would be for men? It would be utter mayhem — industry would fall apart and society would be crumble. Remember how miraculous and strong we women are. Take the glory, as well as the oxygen mask of hormonal help, when your hormones are screaming for your attention.

SECTION 9

MENTAL HEALTH AND MENOPAUSE

One day you're holding it all together nicely. The next, you're crying in the Woolies car park because you can't remember where you parked your car. Here's why it's happening — and some ideas to help you get back on track.

The Science

Estrogen and progesterone aren't just in charge of your cycle. They also moonlight as your mood regulators. Estrogen helps with serotonin — that's your "I've got this" brain chemical. Progesterone supports GABA (or gamma-aminobutyric acid) — the one that keeps you calm and steady. When those hormones start to deplete and glitch, your brain can short-circuit. Cue sudden rage, prickly anxiety, and low mood.

The Big Three

Rage: That fury that suddenly fires up to level 11? That "I've had enough of being taken for granted" feeling? Say hello to your inner dragon.

Anxiety: Racing thoughts, a tight chest, a creeping sense of dread. We feel you, Sister.

The Unravelling: Feeling lost, flat, or invisible, like you've stepped out of yourself and forgotten the way back.

How to Cope

Move: Even a walk around the block counts. Exercise boosts endorphins and clears some of the mental clutter.

The Straight-talking Guide To Menopause

Breathe: Slow, deep breaths help your nervous system calm you down a bit.

Talk: A friend, a therapist, your dog — say the things out loud. You don't have to carry it all alone.

Sleep: Tricky, we know, but naps, routines, and turning off screens before bed can help.

Consider MHT: Menopausal hormone therapy can smooth out the mood swings and lift the fog. Ask your GP — and keep asking until someone listens.

Where to Get Help

If things get really dark — you can't get out of bed, or your thoughts start heading into scary territory — reach out. Call Lifeline (13 11 14) or speak to a psychologist.

Trust us. We've been there. Your spark's not gone, it's just asking for help.

SECTION 10

SEX AND THE PAUSES: YOUR BODY, YOUR RULES

When The Pauses roll in, sex can drop straight to the bottom of the priority pile. And yet, the pressure to care, to perform, to be available doesn't vanish just because your hormones have packed up.

Every woman rides these stages differently.

You might feel a quiet ache — a guilt for the pain and confusion your reduced libido might cause a beloved partner, and a grief for the craving of physical intimacy that once came without a second thought. But you love who you're with and who you are together, so you take honest, informed and loving steps towards regaining the closeness you both miss.

Many of you are choosing to fly solo — because you simply can't manage, balance or struggle with the difficulty of intimate relationships anymore. And you prefer the company and ease of being alone, making your own choices and looking at a future you can design for yourself.

Wherever you land, chances are you're feeling lost and disoriented — caught in a storm of change, an uncertain future-you and the expectations of others.

That said, if the desire for sex still sparks joy and excitement, there are ways to rekindle things on your terms. We've listed a few of them below. Plus you can always talk things through with a medical expert. We've all been there, so we know where you're at.

In life there is always change, and helping each other through that without judgment and with informed solutions is the best way forward.

Whatever you need and whatever works best for you.

Your pleasure. Your pace. Your rules. Always.

What's Changing

Libido: Testosterone takes a dive, stress ramps up, and desire decides to have a little lie-down.

Dryness: Less estrogen means thinner, drier vaginal tissue — which can make sex feel like someone's handed you sandpaper instead of silk.

Comfort: Pain, irritation, or sensitivity can sneak in and kill the vibe. In other words: ouch.

What Helps

Lube: Your new best friend. If you're new to using it or feeling unsure, start with a gentle, water-based lubricant — ideally one that's fragrance-free and designed for sensitive skin. If that dries out too quickly or doesn't offer enough comfort, try a silicone-based one next. In short, if your main concern is comfort and sensitivity, go water based. If your main concern is dryness and endurance, go silicone.

Moisturisers: Not the stuff from your bathroom shelf — look for vaginal moisturisers at the chemist. Use regularly to keep things supple.

MHT: Topical estrogen (pessaries, creams) can restore comfort and pleasure. It's low dose, localised, and safe for most women.

Slow it down: Foreplay's no longer optional — it's essential.

Redefining Intimacy

Intimacy isn't just sex. It never was. It's a closeness. It's togetherness. It's the belly-laugh at an inside joke. It's comfort in a quiet glance. It's being seen.

You might need more time, more care, or simply a new script that's written by you — for a change.

This isn't about getting back to how it was. It's about making room for how it can be. And there's power in that.

SECTION 11

THE MIDLIFE BODY: WHAT'S CHANGING AND WHAT YOU CAN DO ABOUT IT

What used to work might not anymore — and it's not because you've failed, lost control, or 'let yourself go'. It's because your hormones are rewriting the manual. Here's how to take care of the body that's carried you this far — and will carry you further still.

Weight, Metabolism and That Midsection Shift

Your jeans are protesting. The belly bloat is real. The scales? Rude.

Menopause changes how your body stores fat, especially around the middle.

What Helps

Eat smart: Prioritise protein (eggs, tofu, lean meats), fibre (veggies, oats), and less sugar. No starvation — fuel is not the enemy.

Move more: Walking, strength training, dancing in the kitchen — muscle burns more fat, even at rest.

Sleep: We know your sleep schedule can be all over the shop nowadays but if you can get it under control (with MHT or natural remedies) you'll reduce food cravings.

Chill: Cortisol loves chaos. A walk in nature, deep breathing, or yoga helps settle the nervous system.

Bottom line: You don't need to be smaller — you deserve to feel stronger.

Bones

Your skeleton doesn't usually make a fuss — until menopause shows up and estrogen walks off the job. The result? Bones that lose density faster than before, raising the risk of osteoporosis and breaks.

What helps

Calcium-rich foods: Think dairy, tofu, almonds, broccoli, and kale — no need to force down chalky tablets unless your doctor recommends it.

Vitamin D: Get some sunshine or talk to a doctor about supplements if you're low. It helps your body absorb all that bone-loving calcium.

Weight-bearing movement: Walking, light weights, stair climbing — activity makes your bones work and helps keep them solid.

Bottom line: Your bones are the scaffolding of your future. Treat them like the architectural wonders they are.

Heart

When estrogen declines, your heart loses one of its greatest protectors — and cholesterol levels, blood pressure, and risk of heart disease can all sneak up.

What Helps

Quit smoking: If you're still lighting up, now's the time to knock the ciggies on the head.

Alcohol: Consider reducing or quit drinking altogether.

Move daily: Brisk walks, dancing, yoga — your heart loves consistency, not perfection.

Eat heart-loving fats: Avocados, olive oil, nuts, seeds, and oily fish keep your arteries happy. It's not about restriction — it's about nourishment.

Bottom line: Your heart's worked hard for you. Now's the time to return the favour.

Brain

Brain fog is real and — not to scare you — menopause can raise dementia risk in the long term. Don't worry; there's plenty you can do.

What Helps

Challenge yourself: Puzzles, learning something new, reading — your brain loves stimulation.

Prioritise sleep: It's when your brain repairs and resets. Naps count.

Stay social: Laughter, connection, conversation — they keep you sharp, grounded, and sane.

Bottom line: Your brain hasn't failed you — it's just rebooting. Give it time, give it tools, and don't forget to give it credit.

SECTION 12

THE POWER OF LIFESTYLE MEDICINE — MOVEMENT, FOOD, SLEEP, AND SANITY

Now that we've covered how menopause affects your weight, bones, brain and heart, let's talk about other lifestyle tweaks you can make. These habits might not sound sexy, but they're powerful — arguably the strongest medicine you've got. The way you eat, move, sleep and manage stress can either support your body through this transition — or make it harder. Let's make it easier.

Movement: Balance, Not Burn

Forget punishing workouts. In perimenopause and beyond, movement is about preservation. No bootcamp martyrdom required. Try this:

- Strength training 2–3 times a week for muscle and bone
- Walking daily to clear your head
- Yoga for flexibility, sleep and mood
- Dancing to reconnect with joy

Food: Fuel, Not Fear

You don't need to survive on green smoothies and regret. But you do need to eat in a way that supports hormonal stability and energy. Focus on:

- Protein with every meal to curb cravings and support muscle
- Fibre to support gut health and hormone clearance

- Healthy fats (olive oil, avocado, nuts) to nourish brain and hormones
- Complex carbs (sweet potato, oats, legumes) for steady energy
- Avoid ultra-processed foods — not because they're 'bad', but because they can mess with your metabolism, spike inflammation, and leave you feeling like crap.

Sleep: More Precious Than Gold

Getting enough sleep — or avoiding an unbroken night's sleep — can be trickier now. But without enough zees, everything else goes sideways — mood, cravings, immunity, you name it.

- Create a wind-down ritual (no doom-scrolling)
- Try magnesium, sleep stories, or gentle movement
- Keep your room cool, quiet, and dark
- Treat sleep like medicine — because it is
- And yes, time to cut out alcohol.

Stress: The Silent Saboteur

Changes to your cortisol levels mean stored fat, difficulty sleeping, and more anxiety. Managing stress isn't a luxury — it's the work. Start small:

- Breathe
- Walk
- Journal
- Say no
- Laugh
- Sit still

The Takeaway

Menopause is a transition, not a crisis. Your daily habits are the strongest medicine you've got. Not one big fix, but a hundred tiny ones. If you want to feel clearer, calmer, stronger — this is where you start.

SECTION 13

THE INSIDE SKINNY ON MENOPAUSAL HORMONE THERAPY (MHT)

MHT used to be called HRT (Hormone Replacement Therapy) — and it's the gold standard for symptom relief.

MHT replaces the hormones your body's winding down. It can ease hot flushes, brain fog, mood swings, vaginal dryness, sleep issues, and more.

How It's Delivered

Pills, patches, gels, creams — your choice. The dose, delivery, and hormone combo can all be tailored to suit your body and your symptoms.

The Baggage

You've probably heard whispers (or screams) about cancer risks. That stems from older studies that used outdated hormone types and didn't paint the full picture. The result? Decades of fear, confusion, and women being told to just put up with it.

The Study That Shaped the Narrative

In 2002, the Women's Health Initiative (WHI) — a large U.S. study — released results suggesting that hormone therapy increased the risk of breast cancer, heart disease, and stroke. The media ran with it. Women panicked. GPs stopped prescribing it. And millions were left to suffer through severe menopause symptoms with no support.

What went wrong? A lot, actually:

- Most participants were well past menopause — average age 63, many over 70. But hormone therapy is most effective and safest when started closer to menopause (before 60 or within 10 years of your final period). So, the study didn't reflect the women most likely to seek treatment.
- The study used older, synthetic hormones — namely conjugated equine estrogens (made from horse urine) and a synthetic form of progesterone (medroxyprogesterone acetate). These aren't the same as the body-identical hormones commonly used today, which behave much more like your body's own.
- The risks were overstated for individuals. For example, the slight increase in breast cancer risk was similar to that from drinking a glass of wine each night. But the media reported it in ways that made it sound catastrophic.
- Benefits — like reduced risk of osteoporosis, improved quality of life, and relief from debilitating symptoms — were barely mentioned.

Where We Are Now

Newer, better-designed studies show that for most women under 60 (or within 10 years of menopause), MHT is safe, effective, and offers powerful protection. That said, it's not your only option. The next section of this booklet covers alternative and natural therapies, if you fancy taking a different path.

SECTION 14

ALTERNATIVE AND NATURAL THERAPIES

Herbs, supplements, and natural remedies can absolutely pull their weight — but before you splash out on maca, magnesium, or magic capsules, rule out any underlying issues. It's always important to disclose alternative/ natural therapies to your medical team (doctor, nurse or pharmacist). But if you're already on medication, definitely have a quick word with your doctor or pharmacist — just to be on the safe side.

The Useful Shortlist (Based on Science, Not Hype)

Magnesium: A quiet hero. Helpful for sleep, anxiety, muscle cramps, and perimenopausal restlessness. Try magnesium glycinate or citrate for better absorption.

Omega-3 Fatty Acids (Fish Oil): Supports brain health, mood, joints, and inflammation. Essential if you don't eat oily fish.

Vitamin D: Crucial for bones, immune function, and mood. Many women are deficient. You might want to get tested.

Calcium: Important for maintaining bone density, and its effectiveness is amplified by vitamins D and K2. But talk to a healthcare professional about how much is too much.

Probiotics: Supports gut health, immunity, and mood. Helpful for stomach issues or frequent UTIs.

B-Complex Vitamins: These boost your energy, nervous system, and mood. Vital if you're vegan or stressed.

The Maybe List (Some Evidence, Some Hype)

Black Cohosh: The OG of menopause supplements. It's a herb often recommended for hot flushes and night sweats. Some women swear by it; others feel nothing. If it helps you and you're not on medications it might interact with (hello, liver), go for it — with supervision.

Maca Root: An Andean root touted for energy, libido, and hormonal balance. The research is patchy, but some women report feeling more 'themselves' with it.

Red Clover: Contains phytoestrogens — plant-based compounds that mimic estrogen. Results vary. If you're estrogen-sensitive or have had hormone-related cancer, speak to your doctor first.

Evening Primrose Oil: Used for breast tenderness and mood swings. Not a miracle worker, but for some, it takes the edge off.

Ashwagandha: An adaptogen for stress, anxiety, and sleep. Think slow, steady support.

Acupuncture: Not a Supplement but Certainly Supplemental

Traditional Chinese medicine views menopause as an energy transition. Acupuncture can help regulate sleep, mood, hot flushes, and anxiety for some women. Is the evidence conclusive? No. But if it helps you feel better, that matters.

What to Be Wary Of

- Anything promising to 'balance your hormones naturally' in 10 days, without explaining how.
- Products with dozens of unpronounceable ingredients costing a gazillion dollars and listing 'hormone harmony' as their main benefit.
- Supplements sold by influencers claiming their menopause was cured with a shake and three daily capsules of powdered unicorn horn. Unless they're licensed health practitioners, save your money.

A Few Important Caveats

- Start small: Try one supplement at a time to see what helps.
- Track symptoms: Use a journal to note changes.
- Avoid mega-doses: More isn't better. In fact, it may be harmful.
- Look for transparency: GMP-certified, third-party tested brands.

The Bottom Line

There's definitely room for alternative and natural treatments. You don't have to choose one path. You just have to choose what works for you.

SECTION 15

CREATING YOUR MIDLIFE SUPPORT TEAM – WHY YOU SHOULDN'T DO THIS ALONE

Here's the lie we've all been sold: menopause is a private struggle to manage silently with a brave face and maybe a nice cup of chamomile tea. Nope. That ends here. Menopause is a life stage, not a personal failing, and it deserves expertise, community, and real support. You don't need to do this solo. And you shouldn't.

Let's build your midlife A-team.

The Right Doctor

You need a doctor who:

- Listens without dismissing your symptoms as 'just stress'.
- Understands menopause is more than hot flushes.
- Is up-to-date and open to MHT and modern, evidence-based care.
- Refers to specialists when needed.

A Menopause Savvy Doctor

A GP, endocrinologist or gynaecologist with extra training in hormone health will:

- Run the right tests.
- Prescribe hormone therapy if appropriate.
- Tailor treatment to your symptoms and health history.

A Great Pharmacist

Pharmacists can:

- Ensure meds and supplements play nicely together.
- Advise on dosages and application (gels, patches).
- Spot side effects early.
- Offer alternatives when something's out of stock.
- Work with your doctor by informing them of drug supply issues and alternatives.

Work Allies

Someone in your workplace needs to know what's going on. You don't need to share your entire symptom list (like the Sub-Saharan state of your vagina), but you do need support for:

- Flexibility
- Adjusted deadlines
- A fan in the meeting room
- A quiet moment to recalibrate

That could be HR, your manager, or a trusted colleague. Tell someone.

Your Inner Circle

Your ride-or-die crew will:

- Let you vent.
- Bring snacks.
- Understand, "I just can't today."
- Celebrate wins.
- Know when your tone means 'get me out of here'.

Whether it's a sister, bestie, partner, or WhatsApp group — build your circle.

You

At the centre is you — the woman navigating all this while still showing up for work, kids, parents, friends, partner. Be on your own team:

- Speak up.
- Ask for help.
- Get rest.
- Laugh at the madness.
- Stop apologising for anything and everything.

SECTION 16

MENOPAUSE AND MEN — A PARTNER'S GUIDE

A message to the men in our lives: you're not the enemy, but if you're hoping this 'blows over', you're in for a rocky road ahead. Menopause is a whole-body reset, a shift in identity and chemistry that impacts every part of her life, including your relationship.

Here's your crash course in supporting her — and staying connected.

She's Not Mad at You. She's in a Hormonal Blender

Mood instability is a hallmark of perimenopause — tears from nowhere, rage over small things, a flatness that makes everything heavy. She might snap, cry, go quiet. Don't take it personally (unless you left wet towels on the bed again). It's her chemistry, not her character. She's not pushing you away; she's surviving in a body she doesn't recognise.

Sex Might Change. But It's Not the End.

Menopause often brings:

- Lower libido
- Vaginal dryness
- Pain during sex
- Emotional disconnection

This doesn't mean she doesn't love you; her body just needs a new language. Be gentle, patient, and don't pressure. Ask:

- "What feels good right now?"
- "How can we find new ways to connect?"
- "How can I support your comfort?"

Learn about lube. It's your new bestie. And remember that thing called foreplay?

Don't Suggest Getting a Massage – Suggest Getting a Menopause-Literate Doctor

She's not burnt out or 'overly sensitive'. She's likely sleep-deprived, estrogen-depleted, and unsupported. She needs real care — hormone therapy, perhaps — not just pampering. If you really want to earn brownie points, you might even offer to listen in (and learn) when she has her doctor's appointment. THEN book the massage.

Learn. Ask. Show Up

Women have quietly managed hormonal chaos since puberty, hiding the mess to not 'inconvenience' the world. Now, she shouldn't have to do it alone. Read that book, watch that documentary, ask how she's really feeling. If she's withdrawn, keep showing up — be beside her when she needs you, and give her space when she doesn't. Your support doesn't have to be perfect; it just has to be there.

This Is Temporary. Your Partnership Is Not

The hormonal turbulence eases. The fog lifts. Sex returns. Clarity comes back — often better, bolder, freer. If you've weathered the storm with grace, you'll have a woman who trusts you deeply. Nothing says, "I love you," like staying calm during a hot flush, or listening through tears and having empathy and patience for what is a very challenging time. Just remember it's not personal, it's hormonal.

SECTION 17

HOW TO TALK TO YOUR GP AND GET TAKEN SERIOUSLY

Let's start with the maddening truth: menopause is still wildly under diagnosed, under-researched, and under-discussed.

It's no wonder so many women are misdiagnosed with depression or anxiety and handed a prescription for pills. Or dismissed entirely with a shrug and the infuriating, "It's just your age."

You deserve more. This is your guide to navigating the medical maze, so you get the care you actually need.

Prep Before the Appointment

1. **Track your symptoms**, including:
   - Period changes
   - Sleep issues and quality
   - Mood swings, anxiety, rage
   - Hot flushes (time, intensity, triggers)
   - Night sweats
   - Brain fog, memory issues
   - Vaginal/bladder changes
   - Energy
   - Weight changes
   - Food cravings
   - Exercise
   - Joint pain
   - Libido shifts
   - Medications/supplements
   - Alcohol/caffeine/stress/sugar

When you track symptoms, patterns emerge, trends appear, and you stop second-guessing yourself. Use a journal or a spreadsheet. Print it, slap it on the fridge. Tracking takes back your narrative.

2. **Write down your questions**: Ask about perimenopause tests, and mood/weight/sleep/sex support.
3. **Know what treatments interest you**: If you've read about body-identical MHT, mention it. Bring research if needed.
4. **Know your timeline**: When did symptoms start? Are you still menstruating?
5. **Set your top three goals**: For example, better sleep, raising libido, feeling like yourself.
6. **Bring your current meds/supplements**: Transparency avoids adverse reactions.
7. **Consider bringing a support person**: A friend or partner can back you up. Strength in numbers and all that.
8. **Take notes**: Menopause brain fog is real. You don't want to forget stuff.

At the Appointment: Be Your Best Advocate

- **Be Clear:** "I believe I'm in perimenopause and want to explore treatment options."
- **Be Direct:** "Can we discuss MHT and whether I'm a candidate for body-identical hormones?"
- **Be Firm:** If brushed off, ask, "What specifically are we waiting for?"
- **Be Curious:** "If MHT isn't recommended, can you explain why?" You're not there to be polite — you're there to be helped.

If You Hit a Wall

Not all doctors are menopause-literate. Ask for a referral to a specialist or find a new doctor. You're not difficult for asking questions — you're informed. The speediest road to the right solution is in your hands.

What a Good Doctor Offers

- Time
- Respect
- Evidence-based options
- Clear explanations
- A follow-up plan
- Comfort with body-identical MHT

What You Deserve

- To be believed
- To be treated as an equal
- To have symptoms taken seriously
- To be offered real options

After the Appointment

- Book follow-up tests
- Fill prescriptions
- Track treatment responses
- Maybe buy a croissant — advocacy is hard work.

SECTION 18

RED FLAGS AND WHEN TO SEEK HELP

Menopause comes with plenty of body/mind changes but not everything that happens during this time is par for the hormonal course. This is your Red Flag List.

Extremely Heavy or Prolonged Bleeding During Perimenopause

Periods can get weird around about now, but if you're:

- Bleeding through pads hourly
- Bleeding for 10+ days
- Passing large clots
- Feeling faint or exhausted from blood loss

That's not just perimenopause — it's a potential anaemia risk or sign of fibroids, endometriosis, or other conditions.

Bleeding After Menopause

If you've gone 12 months without a period and suddenly start bleeding, it's not a fluke. It needs investigation. Most cases are benign (polyps, thinning tissue), but occasionally it's serious. Don't wait — make an appointment with a medical professional.

Crushing Fatigue That Won't Shift

Menopause fatigue is real, but if you can't get out of bed or are nodding off at work, something else might be at play — thyroid dysfunction, iron deficiency, sleep apnoea, autoimmune flare-ups. Blood tests are recommended.

Sudden Mood Collapses or Intrusive Thoughts

Mood swings are common, but if you experience:

- Prolonged low mood
- Daily crying
- Panic attacks
- Suicidal or intrusive thoughts

That's not 'just hormones', it's mental health, and it's urgent. Help is available through GPs, psychologists, and hormone therapy. Speak up.

Heart Palpitations or Chest Pain

Estrogen affects the heart. Palpitations can be harmless, but chest tightness, pain down the arm, sudden breathlessness, or dizziness need immediate attention.

Ongoing Pelvic or Lower Back Pain

Could be nothing, or it could be endometriosis, fibroids, or a cyst. If it persists, check it out.

Final Note

We've been told to minimise, to 'wait it out', to put everyone else first. What absolute and unmitigated nonsense. Get the help you need — the help you deserve.

SECTION 19

THRIVING POST-MENOPAUSE — YOUR GOLDEN AGE

You've walked through the fire. The sweat-drenched nights. The tearful GP visits. The blood-soaked sheets and soul-sapping fatigue. You've navigated the brain fog, the spreadsheets of supplements, the hormone hacks and the moments you didn't recognise yourself in the mirror. And now? You've made it. You're postmenopausal. Not broken. Not diminished. Transformed.

This isn't the epilogue. This is the beginning of your next masterpiece.

What Changes Now

The storm quiets. The wild hormonal surges flatten out. With estrogen's exit comes a strange and glorious steadiness. You may find:

- A clearer head and sharper focus
- Energy that's no longer feast or famine
- Emotions that no longer ambush you
- A libido that returns on your terms
- And most of all, a sense of ownership over your body, your time, your life.

You'll still need to care for your bones, your heart, your mind — but now it's simply maintenance. You're not guessing anymore. You know your body, and you know your worth.

Thriving Isn't Just Health — It's Purpose

This phase of life brings bold, burning questions. We can't answer them for you. It's your turn to set the 'New You' Agenda. To ask yourself:

- What do I want now?
- Who am I when I'm not defined by fertility, caretaking, or approval?
- What passions did I sideline to be who I was told to be?
- Where am I meant to go next?

This isn't reinvention — it's reclamation. Of time. Of space. Of your voice. Of your story.

You are the result of everything you've survived. Everything you've learned. Everything you've let go of. There's no need to rush. No need to please. You are ready for you. Glorious, strong, balanced and invincible you. What's next is for you to decide. Dream away.

SECTION 20

SUMMARY CHEAT SHEET

For those who skipped ahead or need a recap, here's the short version.

You're Not Crazy. It's Perimenopause.

- Hormones shift years before your final period.
- Mood, sleep, sex drive, weight, memory change.
- Symptoms vary but are real and common.

You Deserve Real Medical Help

- Ask about MHT.
- Demand more than vitamins and better vibes.
- Track symptoms.
- Be clear with your doctor.
- Get a second opinion if dismissed.

Lifestyle Medicine Is Powerful

- Strength training, protein, rest = the holy trinity.
- Magnesium is underrated.
- Alcohol is overrated. Time to reduce drinking or give it up.
- Sleep is sacred.
- Food is medicine.
- Boundaries are therapy.

This Isn't Just About Today

- Menopause affects bones, brain, heart.
- Early support prevents future issues.
- You're not overreacting—you're adapting.

You Need a Support Team

- The right doctors
- Pharmacists

- Work allies
- A hormone-literate bestie
- Yourself

You're Not the Same Woman

- You're wiser
- Less apologetic
- More powerful
- Unstoppable

SECTION 21

A NOTE TO YOUNGER WOMEN — BECAUSE THIS IS FOR YOU, TOO

So, you're not 'there' yet. You're just doing a little recon. Brilliant. Because here's the thing: the earlier you understand what's coming, the less likely you'll be blindsided by it.

We're not here to freak you out. We're here to hand you the map before the terrain starts shifting.

Perimenopause doesn't arrive with a formal invite. It creeps in, subtle at first — maybe your cycle gets weird, your sleep starts playing up, your patience thins, your skin changes, your PMS hits harder. You think it's stress, age, parenting, work. You brush it off.

But knowing what's hormonal and what's not? That's power. Real power.

Here's why it matters:

- You'll learn to spot hormonal shifts early — and respond with clarity, not panic.
- You'll know which tests actually help — and which ones won't tell you squat.
- You'll start protecting your bones, your brain, and your brilliant sense of self before the dip even begins.
- You'll have language for what's happening — which means less shame, more strategy.
- And best of all? You'll be the friend who helps others navigate it too. The one who normalises the weird stuff. Who says, "Hey, I've read about this. You're not going mad."

You don't have to wait until your body's in full hormonal free fall.

You can start now — with cycle tracking, mood mapping, nourishing food, strength-building, and creating a village that talks about this stuff out loud.

This isn't about becoming obsessed with ageing. It's about claiming your trajectory. Rewriting the story. Staying informed so you can stay powerful.

Because menopause isn't an ending. It's just a different kind of becoming. And you? You'll be ready.

SECTION 22

ABOUT UNPAUSE – YOUR MIDLIFE MENOPAUSE CONCIERGE

You've made it this far, so our guess is you might be looking for a bit of extra help. Say hello to UnPause!

UnPause is a telehealth service made up of leading menopause experts. It connects women, wherever they are, with doctors who truly understand menopause. Add to that a smart set of tools and a community of women who are going through the same wild ride, and you've got part science, part sisterhood, and entirely overdue.

UnPause was born from frustration. From the doctors who waved us off with vague advice. From the midnight Googles that left us even more confused. From the supplements that cost a fortune and delivered next to nothing. From being told to 'just breathe through it' — as if menopause were a mood, not a biological reckoning.

Think of us as your menopause concierge. The one who grabs your bags when you're exhausted, and puts them exactly where they need to be. We help with the chaos. We handle the logistics. We anticipate what you need before you even say it.

Whether you're just noticing changes, deep in the trenches, or standing in the ashes of what came before — we're here, walking beside you with clarity, humour, science and sisterhood.

Because here's the truth: there are no trophies for gritting your teeth through it. We are the generation that will not be silent. We'll ask the questions, demand better care, and redefine what it means to be a woman in midlife.

SECTION 23

FINAL WORDS FROM MARY

I'm forever grateful to be female, I knew that 1000% the first time I saw a penis.

Being a woman is far from easy. But the greatest things never are.

For years, I prayed for a daughter. When that dream finally came true and Jamie arrived, a sacred responsibility was born along with her. I wanted her to know the power that women yield and to cherish the feminine spirit in all its: magic, intelligence, beauty, arduousness and miraculousness. I wanted her to know she is not alone. To never shy away from asking for help. To understand that problems are there to be fixed, not avoided.

This is a good reminder for us all. I want all of us to understand how huge a role hormones play throughout so much of our lives in terms of how we look, feel and function.

Whether it's puberty, pregnancy or menopause — hormones are running the show.

Jamie doesn't have a sister and neither do I. But we do have a sisterhood.

And when things get tough, ugly, exhausting and confusing we know we have the Pussy Posse — or if you're menopausal — the Parched Pussy Posse to help us through.

OTHER RESOURCES

Latest Medical Guidelines (Australia, UK, US)

Australia — RACGP Guidelines (2025)

- MHT is first-line for moderate to severe symptoms.
- Body-identical estradiol and progesterone are preferred.
- Vaginal estrogen is safe long-term.
- Women under 60 or within 10 years of menopause are ideal MHT candidates.
- Routine hormone testing isn't required for perimenopause diagnosis.

UK — NICE Guidelines (2025)

- Perimenopause is a clinical diagnosis; blood tests aren't needed over 45.
- MHT is effective and safe for most.
- Non-hormonal therapies (CBT, SSRIs) are options if MHT isn't suitable.
- Individualise risk-benefit discussions.

US — NAMS Guidelines (2025)

- MHT benefits outweigh risks for women under 60 or within 10 years of menopause.
- Transdermal estrogen and micronised progesterone are safest.
- Testosterone can be considered for low libido.
- Emphasis on shared decision-making and updated WHI understanding.

Glossary of Menopause Terms

- **Perimenopause**: Years before menopause when hormones fluctuate. Can last 4–10 years.
- **Menopause**: 12 months after your final period.

- **Post-Menopause**: Years after menopause with stable, low estrogen.
- **Estrogen**: Supports brain, bones, skin, mood, libido.
- **Progesterone**: Works with estrogen, protects uterine lining, aids mood and sleep.
- **Testosterone**: Supports libido, motivation, muscle mass.
- **MHT (Menopausal Hormone Therapy)**: Replaces hormones your body no longer produces.
- **Vaginal Estrogen**: Low-dose therapy for dryness and urinary issues.
- **Hot Flushes**: Sudden heat surges from hormone dips.
- **Brain Fog**: Cognitive symptoms like forgetfulness and lack of focus.
- **Body-Identical Hormones**: Plant-derived, chemically identical to human hormones.

Further Resources

Books

- *The Definitive Guide to the Perimenopause and Menopause* by Dr Louise Newson
- *The New Menopause* by Dr Mary Claire Haver
- *The Menopause Manifesto* by Dr. Jen Gunter
- *The M Word: How to Thrive in Menopause* by Dr Ginni Mansberg
- *Menopausing: The Positive Roadmap to Your Second Spring* by Davina McCall and Dr Naomi Potter
- *Dare I Say It: Everything I Wish I'd Known About Menopause* by Naomi Watts
- *MaryPause* by Mary Coustas

Podcasts

- *The Dr. Louise Newson Podcast*
- *Rage Against The Menopause* with Patrina Jones
- *Very Peri* by Mamamia
- *Rage Against The Vagine* with Em Rusciano
- *Thriving In Menopause* by Prevention Australia
- *You Are Not Broken* with Dr Kelly Casperson
- *We Have A Situation* with Michelle Bridges

Websites

- unpause.com.au
- balance-menopause.com
- mamamia.com.au/resources/very-peri/
  The Very Peri Resource Centre by Mamamia
- menopausefriendly.au

ACKNOWLEDGMENTS

Thank YOU...

Chris Anastassiades — for letting me flood you with endless material and for your stunning ability to make it so much better. Who would have ever thought that Abbotsford State Primary School would have become our creative matchmaker all these decades and projects later.

George Betsis — for being the high-standard, bigger-picture foreman and visionary that you are. You push, and we get further because of it.

Xanthi Kouvatas — for seeing what was possible in the menopause space and for throwing so much dedication and belief behind it.

Dr Natasha Andreadis — you put magic into medicine. Your spirited love of healing is breathtaking. Synchronicity brought us together, and I'm so grateful to have you by my side.

Nanette Fox, my manager — it's been well over three decades of life and art. What a professional and personal ride it has been for the two of us. Thank you for never being a handbrake but always accelerating me towards where I want to go next.

Tess Fox, my publicist — you are a dreamboat and a gun. Your determination to put good things out there is a blessing to everyone you work with. You see value, and you add so much more.

Tanja Perl — I don't know if I've worked with anyone who loves getting things done more than you. Everyone needs a Tanja in their lives. So thankful that we have you!

Kim Zacharia — you literally are a living doll. You ran towards us with such generosity and belief; I appreciate that — and you — so much.

Dr Michael Zacharia — thank you for getting it and adding to it. And thank you for Kim!

Dr Dalia Ubied — your passion for helping women feel their best and do their best is inspiring. So happy we found you.

Nicholas Samartis — your eyes are stars. Thank you for capturing so much in your beautiful photographs, for the many years of friendship, and for the millions of laughs!

Jenny Liu — love that your design DNA is all over our book cover. Thank you for your beautiful taste.

Matt Keon — thank you for your big brain, your support, and for letting us borrow your beautiful dog Mya — indefinitely. So great having you in my inner-circle.

Professor Alex Christou — thank you for your heavyweight belief in me and us — you are an absolute giant.

Julie Postance — thank you for your help in getting this labour of love out into the world. Synchronicity bought us together as mothers and books in publishing!

Cybele Malinowski — for your beautiful front cover photograph.

Thank you also to: Brian Sher, Victoria Kyriakopoulos, Rose Herceg, Di Strang & Nicole Hoyek, Josh & Ali Shields, Selena Hanet-Hutchins, Kirsty & Paul Alexandrou, James Stevens, Genevieve Gregor, Grant Vandenberg, Cheryl Fitzall, Sam Halcroft, Therese Keys, Lucy Walker, Kelly Anderson, Sheryl Carroll, Cristina Baron, Grace Molloy, Mazz Nohra, Dr Vijay Roach, George Dimaris & Karl Landers & Melanie Whitby — for your invaluable advice, talent and support.

And of course, my beautiful family and besties, who fertilise me with love and laughter every single day... my hilarious, one-of-a-kind, and very quotable Mumma; my beautiful witness in life, partner-in-crime brother Con; my brilliant, favourite and very handsome, "Somebody" (and you really are!) And to the Mr Jim and Tina show — one of the best reality sitcoms ever.

And to my Pussy Posse and Besties With Testes — chosen family members — you know who you are... and if you don't, then... Houston, we might have a problem. Yes, I speak of The Bears, The Willis' and every other nonsensical nickname or abbreviated version of your name. I am beyond lucky to have you in my life. Thank you for always keeping me afloat, entertained, fed, and forever ambitious for what's ahead.

ABOUT MARY

For over 35 years Mary Coustas has been a household name and one of Australia's most loved actors, writers, comedians and keynote speakers.

In 1987, she joined the groundbreaking stage show *Wogs out of Work* and in 1989, made her small screen debut as her iconic character Effie in the TV hit Australian sitcom *Acropolis Now*.

Mary has written, starred in, and nationally toured many critically acclaimed one-woman shows including *Waiting for Effie*, *A Date with Effie*, *Love Me Tinder*, *Better Out Than In*, *UpYourselfness* and the hugely successful *Effie the Virgin Bride*. She also found time to write two books: *Effie's Guide to Being Up Yourself* and her deeply personal memoir, *All I Know*, detailing her decade-long, heartbreaking journey to motherhood.

Over the years, Mary has appeared in a wide array of screen and stage roles, including *Hercules Returns*, *Wildside*, *The Secret Life of Us*, *Strife* and *Sunny Nights*. She even played a dog in the Sydney Theatre Company's production of *Sylvia*.

In 2022, right in the depths of menopause, Mary starred in her critically acclaimed first ever Mary one-woman show, *This Is Personal*, at the Sydney Opera House. In 2023 she reached the grand finale of 'Dancing With the Stars', thanks a little to Effie... and a lot to M.H.T.

More about Mary

'*This is Personal…* is not all serious. The naked self-reflection is punctuated by big, loud, roaringly funny scenes of family life, conjured up by Coustas with a mixture of physical theatre and masterful comic timing.'

~ *Harriet Cunningham, Sydney Morning Herald*

'*This is Personal* brings together the skills of storyteller, inspirational speaker, actor and high-octane physical comedian. Entertainment at its best, with a soft underbelly and a kick in its tail.'

~ *Australian Stage*

'Mary Coustas is one of this country's rare and special talents and this is a show in which she shares all of them generously.'

~ *City Hub Sydney*

'Watching *Wogs Out of Work* [1988]… I have previously seen audiences consciously extend goodwill to performers; never before, however, have I seen one barrack for them.'

~ *Martin Flanagan, The Age*

'Splendid characterisation from Mary Coustas, biting commentary on topical issues and even moments of profound pathos…'

~ *Doug Anderson, Sydney Morning Herald*

'Mary Coustas's "Monster" creation, Effie who emerged from the early "Wog" shows of the 1980's has long since passed into legend. She's not just a mere character, this young Greek boofhead from Broadmeadows is a cultural icon.'

~ *Steven Carroll, Sunday Age*

Don't believe a word Mary said about me. She was in a meno haze.

~ *George*

www.ingramcontent.com/pod-product-compliance
Lightning Source LLC
Chambersburg PA
CBHW042318090526
44583CB00025BA/3135